3 Good Choices:

Change It, Accept It, or Leave It

A Woman's Guide to Self-Empowerment

Susan L. Farrell, MBA

SLF PUBLISHING • LEBANON, WI

Copyright ©2018 Susan L. Farrell. All Rights Reserved.

No part of this book may be reproduced or transmitted in any form or by any means, electronic or mechanical, including photocopying, recording, or by any information storage and retrieval system, without written permission of the author, except for the inclusion of brief quotations in a review. For permission, contact the author at **info@susanlfarrell.com**.

ISBN: 978-0-9889090-4-5

First Edition

Published by SLF Publishing, P.O. Box 172, Lebanon, WI 53047

Cover and interior design by AbandonedWest Creative, Inc.

IMPORTANT DISCLAIMER

The purpose of this book is to encourage the reader to think about her or his actions and to make changes if she or he wants to do so. It is based primarily upon the author's experiences. It is not intended to give advice. The author and SLF Publishing shall have neither liability nor responsibility to any person or entity with respect to any loss or damage caused, or alleged to have been caused, directly or indirectly, by the information contained in this book. If you do not wish to be bound by the above, you may return this book to the publisher for a full refund.

This book is dedicated to my mother, Leola (Hill) Farrell. She has been instrumental in helping me realize from a very early age that women have many choices in their lives. These choices can include saying "no" to traditional roles for women such as wife and mother.

Contents

   Foreword 9
   Introduction 13
1 **Getting Started** 19
2 **Change It** 27
3 **Accept It** 71
4 **Leave It** 103
5 **Poor Choices** 125
6 **Rights and Responsibility** 143
   Conclusion 157
   Author's Note 161
   Acknowledgments 163
   About the Author 165

What do you do?
Why do you do it?
Do you want to change?

You have the power within you to become the person you want and to create the life you desire.

Self-empowerment is giving yourself permission and taking responsibility to achieve it.

Foreword

"I walked on through profound darkness with no clear path ahead, knowing full well that, even then, what happened next was my choice."

SHANNON CROTTY

WHEN I STARTED Polka Dot Powerhouse in 2012, under the safety net of another company, I knew nothing about the industry. Nothing. The only thing I knew was that I was dragging a lot of baggage on my back while I was trying to figure it out. The baggage was in the form of past hurts, doubt, fear, and criticism. The immense weight of my load caused me to pause more often than move ahead, and that was okay with me. As long as this new venture of mine stayed small, minimal, and insignificant, I could handle the load. I could continue to bear the weight, without questioning why or whether it was even worth carrying. I could continue in the minimizing story I had built for myself. That was what I knew, and that was where it was safe.

Isn't it funny how things don't always go as we plan? When it became evident that PDP was going to be a stand-alone, worldwide company and much bigger and more important than I had ever imagined, I knew something had to give. I could not genuinely impact the thousands of lives of our members while carrying those heavy cases of sludge. I had two choices. Both made me nauseous. One would keep me safe, but unfulfilled. The other would make me vulnerable in more ways than I could have imagined. It would require me to walk through the high flames of fear and the darkness of the unknown on a daily basis. It was a choice of giving up on the continual growth of the company or throwing off the bags, writing a new story, and walking into my true self.

In the end, the choice I needed to make wouldn't leave me alone until I took decisive action. It kept me awake at night and affected my focus during the day. Like most items of importance in our lives, it would not be ignored, and it waited impatiently for me to make up my mind.

The ability to make the choice required courage and strength and muscles I never knew I had. Miraculously, they showed up at the perfect time. It may have been the heavy responsibility of knowing my sister Tina had sent me the name for the company from heaven, or possibly the countless testimonials we were receiving about the impact our company was having on people's lives. More than that, my gut knew. It always knows. From day one and even through this writing, it never stops say, "Keep going. Millions of people need this."

So, like many of you who will read this, I chose to make the scariest choice possible. And you know what? While it's still very frightening most days and while I often don't know where it will lead, it is one of the most valuable and extraordinary choices I have ever made. This is true for both me and for countless others whom the decision affected.

One big choice leads to a billion others, and the process never ends. Every day we are our own navigational system, relying on faith and belief rather than science and coordinates. It's a miracle that we are able to accomplish extraordinary things in our time on this planet. And yet we do. It happens every day, all over the world. Someone somewhere makes a big scary choice, and the world changes. And changes again.

Once you witness that making a choice gives you strength and freedom and opens new doors that were once locked tight, it gets addictive. You learn to use fear as fuel, and that fuel becomes the ignition switch for what lies ahead for you professionally and personally. You've made it through 100% of your bad days so far. It's impossible to fail. Even if a choice turns out to be wrong, it may lead you down a new and possibly more exciting path. Or it will take you the long way back around to the place you made it so you can choose again. If you make the wrong choice, it may delay you, but it won't stop you. The truth is, if you are truly passionate, driven, and persistent, nothing can.

I am no longer afraid of making a choice. I know there are many only I can make. I won't rest until they're made. I realize I am often my company's and my own bottleneck when I take too long to make one. So now, I educate myself, listen to the opinions of those I trust, consult my gut, and pray…and then, without question, fear, or regret, I make the choice. And I never look back. Back is not where I'm headed.

Choices say a lot about us. They tell people how dedicated we are, what we stand for, and whom we stand with. Maybe most important, they show the world and us how we brave the darkness of the unknown.

As for me, I carry a spotlight and I'm ready to go. I hope this book will act as a tool you can use to build your own spotlight to help guide you on the exciting journey ahead. Let's go!

Shannon Crotty
CEO/Founder Polka Dot Powerhouse

Introduction

    I started my career in long-term care as a foodservice director at a 150-bed nursing home. Less than a year after starting I was promoted to a division dietitian position. Translation: I consulted at several of the company's facilities. I was in that position less than a year when my supervisor, the division coordinator for dining services, asked if I could meet her for lunch. Of course, I agreed. I was not even worried about the meeting because she (let's call her Jane) had never indicated that she had any concerns about my work performance.

    After we placed our lunch orders, Jane told me she was resigning. I was sad to see her leave, but I also thought the next part of the conversation would be whether I was interested in taking her position as division coordinator. In my mind, I was the logical choice. I had been with the company longer than the other division dietitian and had multi-facility experience that the facility dietitians did not.

I was wrong.

I realized my error when she asked if I knew of anyone outside the company who would be interested in the position. I blurted out, "What about me?" She paused then replied that she and her boss (let's call him John) had discussed me. They had decided they were not going to offer me the position because I was too negative.

I was stunned.

Have you ever had a situation in which the world seemed to stand still? That was what happened to me. It was like a movie where all action and sound stopped. My mind, though, was working at warp speed.

At first, I could not understand how they could think I was negative. I did a great job, and the dietary managers and administrators respected and liked me.

After thinking a little deeper, I realized what must have caused their perspective. At meetings, I spoke up and voiced my concerns. In my mind, I was not being negative: I was identifying obstacles that needed to be overcome. Apparently, they did not view it that way.

The first option to address this situation that came to my mind was that I would have to **accept** that I was not going to get this promotion and likely would not get another promotion. I would have to accept that I was not going to advance. I would need to accept that, less than two years out of my dietetic internship, I had reached the pinnacle of my career and was not going any further.

I could not accept that. I had worked too hard to stagnate now. I had picked this company largely because of the opportunity for advancement. No, accepting that my career would not advance was not an option.

If I could not accept the situation, the next option I thought of was to **leave**. I could leave and go to another company where I could advance. I could start over. I did not want to do that, though. Overall, I liked the company. I liked what I did, and I liked my co-workers. I even liked Jane and John.

The third option that occurred to me was that if I did not want to accept staying in my current position forever, and I did not want to leave the company, maybe I could **change** the situation.

How could I change the situation? By changing the perception that Jane and John had of me.

How could I change their perception? By changing my behavior.

I decided I would always be ultra-professional. I decided I would continue to speak up, but I would be much more tactful in how I expressed myself.

All these thoughts took only a few seconds, even though it felt like hours. I decided I would immediately start being ultra-professional. And the professional thing to do was to support the decision. I told Jane that if I thought of anyone who might be interested, I would tell her.

A few weeks later, there was a meeting with the dietitians. Jane had not yet arrived, and the rest of us were talking. Most of the others were complaining about how an outsider was going to be hired for Jane's position. (They thought they were suitable candidates, as I thought I was.) Part of me wanted to join in the complaining. Instead, I stuck with what I had been doing since Jane and I met and did what was professional: I supported the decision. I said that it could be beneficial to have someone with new ideas and who had worked with different procedures and systems to have the position. It might make us more efficient and effective.

As I was finishing, I glanced over my shoulder. Jane was standing just outside the doorway to the meeting room. There was no way she could not have heard.

A few weeks after that, the new person started. She started on Monday. I met her on Tuesday. She resigned on Wednesday. (No, it did not have anything to do with meeting me.) Jane offered me the position on Thursday. I accepted on Friday.

When Jane offered me the position, she said that she and John had noticed a change in my behavior and now thought I would be good in the position. (I realized that by then I might also have looked like the lesser of the evils, but I could live with that.) I stayed with the company for 12 more years and had multiple promotions, including the highest in the discipline, the executive director position.

THE MEETING WITH Jane was an epiphany. Like an explosion in my mind, I knew that we all have three good choices in any situation. We can accept it, leave it, or change it. I have used this philosophy for years, and it has worked.

What I have found over time, though, is that generally I try to change the situation first. I think that is usually the best first step. If the situation is not what I like, why not try to change it?

If I cannot change it, or decide that it is not worth the time or effort to change it, then I determine whether I can accept it. Sometimes accepting it is the best answer. Many times it is just not that big of a deal.

If I cannot change it or accept it, then the only option left is to leave the situation.

None of these decisions is right or wrong. It depends upon the situation, and it depends upon what is right for us. It depends upon who we are, who we want to be, and what we want in life. By consciously thinking of these three options and analyzing each, we can make better decisions for ourselves.

Of course, there are other choices, but they are not good ones. They are not productive or effective ones because they do not accomplish anything positive. We can choose to do nothing, complain, give up, or choose any number of negative and self-destructive behaviors.

A problem with negative choices is that they frequently keep us stuck in the situation. We allow the situation to control us. We give it power over us. It is only after we change, accept, or leave the situation that we can move forward. It is only then that we control the situation. It is only then that we have power over the situation.

We are always making choices. At the minimum, we are choosing to do something or choosing to do nothing—it is still a choice. It is better if we choose to do something positive.

Although my epiphany was "accept it, leave it, or change it," I decided for the purposes of the book to change the order of discussion to "change it, accept it, or leave it." This is the order that I most frequently use and the order that I think makes the most sense and gets the best results.

This book provides thoughts and stories on each choice: change it, accept it, or leave it. It is my hope that it will assist you in making the choices that are best for you.

Getting Started 1

ONE WAY TO use this book is to simply read it. Another way, and one that will probably be more beneficial, is to think about how you can use the information as you read. To make this easier, I have included exercises throughout the book to encourage you to think and for you to write your thoughts and ideas.

I have organized this book to discuss three basic situation categories: professional, personal, and overall wellness. Within each of these categories there are external and internal factors.

Professional situations are, of course, those related to your career or job. They include specific items such as the profession or industry, position or job responsibilities, and the company for which you work.

Personal situations are everything else. They include

specific areas such as our marital/partner status, parenthood (or not), social and community activities, interests and hobbies, and all the things that we do when we are not at work. These are the things that enrich our lives, make them more rewarding, and/or allow us to express ourselves in ways that are not possible professionally.

Although it is not possible to separate our professional and personal lives (we have just one life, after all), I separated them here as a method of organization. There are many things, though, that fit into and affect both. For example, our health impacts everything in our life. We all have the same amount of time, and we each decide how to spend it. Our financial situation impacts all aspects of our life. We have multiple relationships, professional and personal, in our life. Our lifestyle is a combination of our professional and personal life. For lack of a better descriptor, I included these under an "overall wellness" category.

Any situation within each of these categories (professional, personal, and overall wellness) will contain external factors and internal factors. External factors are those things outside of us. Internal factors are those things inside of us.

External factors are those things outside of us that affect us. Examples of external factors include the skills and knowledge to do a job, volunteer position, or hobby. It includes financial compensation, if any. It includes the workplace environment. The economic environment, whether local or global, is an external factor. Another external factor is how others view us and interact with us. Although we can sometimes influence external factors, we cannot control them.

Internal factors are those things that are inside of us, inside our hearts and minds, that make us who we are. Examples of internal factors include our thoughts, beliefs, values, personality traits, behavioral choices, emotional issues, and personal history. We have control over our internal factors. We can choose and change most of these things. For example, we can choose to focus on the positive rather than the negative. For those that we can't change, such as our personal history, we can choose to change how we view it, how we manage it, and how it affects us. It might not be easy, but it is possible.

External and internal factors can overlap considerably. Our thoughts, beliefs, and other internal factors can be directly related to our perception of external factors. (Remember that our perception is our reality.)

When we are looking at a situation, it can be beneficial to examine both external and internal factors. For example, if you don't like your job, is it because of external factors such as the work environment or pay? Or is it because of internal factors such as believing you are not qualified to do the job or that the job is beneath you?

The exercises for this chapter are to help you think about situations in your life that you would like to address. Consider professional, personal, and overall wellness situations or issues. The purpose of these exercises is to help you think about situations with which you are not satisfied. Exercises in subsequent chapters will assist you in deciding if it is best to change, accept, or leave the situation.

Write down any situations that concern you. On the professional level it might be that the profession or industry that you are in is not what you thought it would be or is no longer satisfying. Your position or job responsibilities might not be satisfactory. Perhaps you and the company are not a good fit. Maybe you do not have the opportunity for advancement or you need more flexibility in your schedule. Maybe you don't believe you are able or allowed to do the job to your satisfaction. List both external and internal factors. Be as detailed as possible.

For example, in my epiphany story, the situation was primarily my relationship with two people, my supervisor and her supervisor. To change the situation of not getting promoted, I needed to change how they perceived me (external). To change their perception, I had to change my behavior (internal).

On the personal level, perhaps you would like to change your relationship status or the quality of your relationship. Perhaps you are not a parent but would like to become one. Maybe you are interested in traveling but do not have the resources. Perhaps you would like a more active social life. Perhaps you would like to start or spend more time on a hobby or volunteering. Maybe you have what you want but don't believe you deserve it. Or you have what you thought you wanted and are still not happy. Write down everything that comes to mind. Include both external and internal factors.

Think about the overall wellness items. Are your health, appearance, finances, relationships, and lifestyle satisfactory? Are you spending your time the way you want? Are there any internal factors (thoughts, beliefs, behavioral choices) that are hindering you? If there is anything with which you are not satisfied, write it down.

In all the categories, do not limit yourself to my examples. I am certain that there are many things that people want to improve that will never occur to me.

There are not any right or wrong answers. This is to assist you in thinking about aspects of your life that you want to address.

Exercise 1-1
What professional situations do I want to address?

Situation	External Factors	Internal Factors

Exercise 1-2
What personal situations do I want to address?

Situation	External Factors	Internal Factors

Exercise 1-3
What overall wellness situations do I want to address?

Situation	External Factors	Internal Factors

1
GETTING STARTED

Change It 2

IF THERE IS something in our lives that we are not happy with, why not try to change it? What do we have to lose? If changing it does not work, we can always decide to accept it, or if the situation is really bad, leave it.

In each category, common situations that concern most people are discussed. Most of these are external factors. At the end of each category are common internal factors. It is not meant to be a comprehensive list. I am sure there are situations that you want to address that are not discussed here. And even if the general situation is addressed, you probably have your own set of external and internal factors to consider.

Professional Situations
- **PROFESSION/INDUSTRY**

Sometimes the profession or industry that we are in does not seem to be a good fit for us. One of the first things to determine is whether it truly is the profession or if it is our job within that profession. For example, a nurse who wants to provide care for people might be frustrated in a role that is primarily administrative. Conversely, a nurse who is burned out on direct care might find an administrative position, where she can use her knowledge in a different way, a welcome change. In each case, nursing is still a good profession for each woman. It's just the position within that profession that is causing dissatisfaction.

If you have invested a great deal of time, money, and effort in obtaining the education, experience, and licensing necessary to work in a particular profession, it would be worthwhile to first look at other opportunities within that profession. There might be a relatively simple change that you can make to increase your satisfaction with your profession. The change might be a new position, perhaps advancement with your current employer, or a position with a new employer.

If there is nothing in your current profession that interests you or that you would enjoy doing, then a way to change it would be to obtain the degree necessary to change to a new profession or industry. This, of course, entails additional time, money, and effort, but it might be worth it. If you and your employer have a good relationship, the company might help you with starting a new career if you can demonstrate how that will help the company.

I have never been dissatisfied with a profession I have been in, but my professions have changed over the years.

I started as a registered dietitian specializing in healthcare foodservice management. I worked for 14 years for a national long-term care company, continually moving up the career ladder. I started as a foodservice director and left as the executive director of dining services.

After I left, I started my own consulting business, SLF Consulting & Training, LLC. I assisted long-term care clients with cost control, customer satisfaction, and regulatory compliance. During this time someone suggested that I speak and give presentations to increase business. It sounded like a good idea, so I did.

I discovered that I liked speaking on foodservice management more than consulting. My business became more speaking and less consulting. I gradually started speaking about self-empowerment topics in addition to foodservice management. When someone suggested I write a book to gain credibility, I decided that sounded like a good idea as well.

When my first book was published, I found I liked being an author even better than being a speaker. Writing on self-empowerment has been my focus since.

I offer this story as an example of how our careers can evolve. We can use what we learned in one profession in other professions, and often these professions overlap. If you do not like your current profession, investigate to see how it can take you to where you want to go. Always keep your eyes open for new opportunities.

▪ POSITION/JOB RESPONSIBILITIES

You might like your profession but are not happy in your current position or role. Something to determine is whether it is the work and responsibilities related to the position or if it is the company for which you work that is causing dissatisfaction.

If it is the position, perhaps it is possible to change the position itself, or perhaps it is possible to change to a new position within the company. Both possibilities are worth investigating.

If it is the company, then a possible change is to find a similar position with a different employer.

Maybe you like the position in that you like what you do, but you need more flexibility related to caring for children, elderly parents, a disabled spouse, or to meet your own health needs. Would it be possible to work from home certain days? Would it be possible to work different days, such as weekends instead of during the week? Would it be possible to go to work early and leave early? Or go late and stay late? Is there a way to make the position part-time? Could you job-share with someone else who also needs more flexibility?

> Sometimes you can create the job you want by analyzing what needs to be done and taking initiative. My role when I was hired for a part-time position for a foodservice company was vague. It was to help a certain group of customers so that my supervisor could focus on other responsibilities.
>
> By assessing what could benefit these customers beyond what they were currently receiving and comparing that to what I could offer them in the way of training and other resources, I created a rewarding position for myself and a greater resource than these customers had ever had. My hours continued to increase as well as my reputation within the company.

Once, a friend was in a very difficult situation. It is not worth going into all the office politics involved, but basically someone talked my friend's supervisor into giving him my friend's position. The supervisor told my friend, on a Friday afternoon, that he did not want to fire him, but he did not know what to do with him.

My friend spent the weekend thinking about his strengths, what his ideal job would be, and how he could best benefit the company. He met with his supervisor on Monday with a detailed plan for a completely new position. His supervisor loved it. My friend continued to grow and be very successful within the company, surpassing the person who acquired his old position.

- **COMPANY/EMPLOYER**

Maybe your dissatisfaction stems from the company that employs you. The company culture might not fit with your values. You can try to change the culture, but realistically that may not happen.

Maybe you want more money, recognition, responsibility, or advancement. Start by telling your supervisor what you want. If you don't, she will never know. Then ask her what you need to do to obtain what you want. Don't expect your employer to just give you what you want. It might happen, but usually if you want more, you need to give more. Also, share what you have already done to merit what you want. Your supervisor might not have noticed your contributions. If the opportunities are not available in your department, perhaps a transfer to another department or segment of the company is a possibility.

Maybe the reverse is true. You want less responsibility or less work. Again, talk to your supervisor about possibilities. Keep in mind, though, that if you want to do less, it is reasonable for your employer to want to pay you less.

Perhaps you do not like where the company is located. Perhaps you have a long commute. It might be possible to change the situation by working from home a certain number of days.

> In one position I held, I liked the profession, the position, and the company. What I did not like was one aspect of my supervisor. She expected me to lie to customers. The first time she told me to lie to cover her, I was so shocked I did it. I immediately regretted it. The second time, she told me to prepare to lie if a certain situation occurred. I decided I was not going to do it, but since the situation did not occur, I did not have to confront her with my decision. By the third occasion that she told me to lie I was ready and told her, "No. I am not going to lie for you."
>
> I think she was shocked that I told her no. She did, however, backtrack and say that that was not what she had meant. She then left my office. She never told me to lie for her again. In that case, I changed the situation by confronting her. Sometimes confrontation is necessary for change to occur.

▪ INTERNAL FACTORS

If you are not satisfied with your professional life, are external factors the primary issue? Or internal?

One of the first things to consider is your thoughts and beliefs related to having a job or career. Do you view it as an important part of who you are, or is it something you'd rather not do but must to pay the bills?

> I got my first job when I was 12. It was feeding calves at a baby-beef operation where my parents were managers. At that time in Wisconsin, if you worked for or with your parents and worked in agriculture, child labor laws were lenient.
>
> I loved it. I was thrilled to be making minimum wage. It was much more than what I earned as an allowance for doing chores at home and more than I could make babysitting. Plus, I preferred taking care of animals to children. I had money to buy the clothes I wanted to wear, rather than being dependent upon what my mother wanted to buy for me. I had money to buy the books I wanted. Having a job made me feel fantastic. It was worth the long hours of dirty, difficult, and tiring physical labor.
>
> From a very early age, work meant independence and self-sufficiency. It still means that to me. I have always preferred working and having my own money to being dependent upon someone else to take care of me. My core values include responsibility, independence, and self-sufficiency. Having a job enables me to live these values. Having a career enables me to live another value, making a difference.

On one end of the spectrum, there are women who love having a job or career. It is an extremely important part of who they are. On the other end of the spectrum, there are women who not only do not want a job, but do not think they should have to have a job. They believe someone else should take care of them, provide for them, and pay their way. (Of course, there are women throughout the spectrum as well.)

Think about the two belief systems in play here. If a woman who loves to work is dissatisfied with her job, it might be because of external factors. If a woman who doesn't want a job is dissatisfied with her job, it might be because of internal factors. It might not be possible for her to be satisfied with any job until she changes her thoughts and beliefs about having a job first.

There are also women who find themselves with conflicting values. They enjoy having a job or career, they enjoy caring for their family, but there doesn't seem to be enough time to do both well. This can be especially difficult if they feel that family, friends, and society are pushing them toward what they "should" do. By looking at all the internal factors at play, it can become easier to determine what is causing the dissatisfaction. It might not be about the job, but about balance or unrealistic expectations.

Another set of beliefs about work concerns getting what you want. Some believe that to get what you want, you need to work for it. Others believe that they should get what they want just because they want it. The first group is more likely to get what they want than the second. Why? Because they act to get what they want, while the second group waits for someone to give it to them. Changing beliefs can change outcomes.

A possible internal factor is burnout. Maybe you used to love what you did, and you don't anymore because of burnout. If that is the case, consider getting help from a therapist, career counselor, or someone else who can assist you in overcoming this.

Other internal factors could be what we believe about ourselves in relation to our jobs. Some people feel that they are in over their heads and are not qualified to do a job. Others feel that they are overqualified for a job and that their talents are wasted. In either case, changing jobs might not help. Addressing these internal factors might.

As long as we do not harm ourselves or others, there are not any right or wrong beliefs related to work. However, if you are not satisfied with your professional life, first examine your thoughts and beliefs related to having your job and/or career. Could these internal factors be causing your dissatisfaction? If you changed your thoughts, would it change the situation for you?

Personal Situations
- **RELATIONSHIP STATUS**

An extremely important part of our personal life is, for lack of a better term, our "relationship status." I am using that term to include everything from being single, to dating, to being in a committed relationship, to being married, and everything in between and beyond.

We may be in a situation where we like the "status" (for example, married) but not the "relationship" (for example, the quality of the marriage).

If we are not happy with one of these (or both) it is possible to make changes. The first step is to determine exactly what we have, what we like, what we don't like, and the changes we need to make.

An important question to ask in this and in every situation is: Why? Why do we want to be dating? Why do we want to be married? Why are we marrying this person? Is it because it truly is best for us, or is it because family, friends, or society are telling us that this is what we should want?

An even better question than "Is this best for me?" is "Is this best for me at this point in my life?" For example, would it better to get an education and start a career first? Would it be better to develop into the person you want to be first? If you are considering marriage (or re-marriage), these are important questions to ask yourself before making a decision.

Another important aspect is to define what the relationship that you want means to you and then look for someone who wants the same thing. For example, if you want a career, don't marry someone who wants a wife for cleaning, cooking, and childcare. Marry someone who will consider your career as important as his rather than as a hobby that you do in your "free" time.

> It took me a long time to determine what marriage means to me. Finally, I determined that for me, marriage needs to be an equal partnership. I want to be an equal partner to him, and I want to be treated as such. I want him to be an equal partner to me. What he wants is just as important to me as it is to him. What I want needs to be just as important to him as it is to me. We work together to create an equal partnership. The opposite of that is a double standard, where it is all about one person.

If you want to change your status, determine why and then how. If you want to change the relationship, read the section on relationships under "Overall Wellness Situations" for ideas. There are also many books available that address this subject. Depending upon your situation, you may also want to seek professional assistance.

When I was divorced and dating, I realized something very important. Our freedom has value, too. When we are single, we have the freedom to do what we want, when we want, with whom we want, for as long as we want. We are only responsible for ourselves. When we enter a committed relationship, we lose that freedom. We need to consider the other person as much as ourselves. We have a responsibility to him or her as well. Before you exchange your freedom for a relationship, be sure that the relationship has at least the same value as your freedom.

- **PARENTHOOD (OR NOT)**

If you do not have children, and want children, in many cases that is a change that can be made. If you cannot easily have your own, then medical assistance might be necessary. If that does not work, then there might be the possibility of adoption, being a foster parent, step-parent, or other ways to involve yourself with children.

An extremely important question to ask yourself before deciding to become a parent is: Why? Why do you want children? Why do you want to be a parent? Why do you want to be a parent now?

Do your answers truly reflect who you are? Or do they reflect what family, friends, and society think you should be?

Are your reasons good ones for the child? Do you want to be a parent because you want to accept the responsibility that goes into being a good parent? Or do you want a child because it seems like all your friends have them? Or that you want someone to love you? Or that you want a best friend?

Do you feel that having a child would improve the quality of your relationship with your partner? Or that having a child would solidify your relationship if you want to move to the next level but your partner is hesitant? Are you afraid that your partner will leave you and if you have a child he will stay? These are not good reasons to have a child. It is not fair to your partner, and it is not fair to the child.

There are many poor reasons to have a child. Since the child is going to pay the highest price if you make a poor choice, be sure that if you decide to have a child, it is for the right reasons. That is, you want to be a responsible, nurturing parent.

If you already have children, and do not want them, there is not much you can legally do to change that. (I'm attempting to be humorous. The parents I know would never give up their children. Some, occasionally, on really bad days, however...)

You might be in a situation where you want to change the relationship that you have with your children. There are many parenting books available. You might also want to seek professional help. A more positive relationship will not only help you, it will also help your children.

▪ INTERESTS

Our interests include social and community activities, hobbies, volunteering, and all the things that we enjoy doing. They may be something as simple as reading or watching movies or as complex as building furniture. Sometimes hobbies, given time, even become businesses.

If we are not satisfied with any of our interests, making a change is usually low risk. There are many things, such as volunteering, that require only our time. It's easy to do different social activities. If we want to start a new hobby, we can probably do so with minimal financial or time commitments. If we find we enjoy it, we can invest more in it. Some interests, such as travel, may require a greater financial investment, but that is something for which we can save.

Changing your interests is easy to do, and it is easy to change back if you want. Sometimes making a small change like this can have a big impact on the enjoyment you have in life.

▪ INTERNAL FACTORS

Remember that external factors come from outside of you and internal factors come from inside of you. It can be difficult to separate them sometimes.

The previous discussion on relationship status and parenthood incorporated many questions to encourage you to think about internal as well as external factors. A major external factor is when other people try to influence you to do what they think you should do. Just because they think you should does not mean that it is right for you.

It is important to separate what is external (what others think) and internal (what you think). Once you have, an additional step is to ask yourself where your thoughts and beliefs originated. Once you realize where they came from, you can decide whether it makes sense to change them.

For example, if your ideas of marriage are based on what your parents had, does that make sense for who you are? Or do you want to create new beliefs on what marriage means to you? If your beliefs on what it means to be a mother are based on what your mother did, does that make sense for who you are and what is happening in the world now? Or do you want to create a new set of beliefs on what it means to be a parent? Maybe deep inside you know parenthood is not for you, but there is so much pressure to have children that it is difficult to believe in yourself in this matter. Professional help can assist in areas like this.

Consider internal factors when it comes to interests as well. Are there reasons you do or don't do certain things?

> I spent most of my life not volunteering. I'd give a little to charities sometimes, but that was it. I never thought I had the time to do it, and I didn't really see the benefit to myself or others. I didn't think the little time I might be able to give would make a difference.
>
> It wasn't until I was in my 50's that I finally started volunteering, and even then I started for selfish reasons. I had always had cats, and my last one had passed away in April one year. I wanted to get two kittens, but I wanted to wait until we returned from vacation in June. It was a good plan, except that I really needed a "feline fix" before June.
>
> I started volunteering at the local humane society that April. I went in about once a week to help socialize the cats to make them more comfortable with people and thus more adoptable. When I returned from vacation, the director asked if I would like to foster a mother cat and her seven kittens. (We ultimately adopted three of the kittens.) I have been fostering since as well as continuing to help socialize and find homes for the cats at the humane society.
>
> What I have found is that what little I do does make a large difference in the lives of the cats I interact with. If everyone would just do a little, it would make an impressive difference in the world as well. I have also personally benefitted from it. It feels good to do good.

Often we don't try new things because of fear. If fear is an internal factor holding you back from something you would like to do, ask yourself this: What is the worst thing that could happen, and would it really be all that bad?

Overall Wellness Situations
- HEALTH

An area in which many of us want to make changes is our health. Although good health is important at any age, the importance becomes more evident as we get older and discover our bodies are not as indestructible as we once thought. In addition to our physical health, we also have to be concerned with our mental and emotional health.

To change our health, we have to change aspects of our lifestyle. In general, we usually need to eat healthier and exercise more. If we have unhealthy habits such as smoking or excessive drinking, we need to stop. Misuse of drugs can cause serious problems and is not limited to illegal drugs. Prescription medications can be very dangerous if misused.

A recommendation I want to emphasize is to seek help from medical professionals for any major health concerns. Start with your primary doctor. Ask for references or referrals to specialists as needed. There are many people selling health information without any qualifications to do so. Many just want to make money. Some may have good intentions, but that does not mean that they have the knowledge to determine if what they are selling is healthy overall, let alone healthy for you with your unique health concerns. Remember, there is no magic pill to give you what you want. If what someone says seems too good to be true, it probably is.

Lifestyle health habits can be some of the most difficult changes of all. However, these changes are critical if we are to improve or even maintain our health. And the sooner we make these changes, the greater impact they will have on our lives.

■ APPEARANCE

Many of us are concerned with our appearance. Too many of us are probably overly concerned with our appearance. However, in our society, appearance matters in that people judge us based upon how we look. It doesn't mean that it is right, but it is true. The decision each of us must make is the extent to which we care.

> I have decided that as long as I am healthy, well-groomed, look professional for the situation, and like what I see when I look in the mirror, I'm good. This doesn't mean that I don't do things to improve my appearance. I use skin and haircare products to maximize what I have. I color my hair. I wear makeup if I'm going out. I eat healthy most of the time and exercise frequently. I buy clothes that fit well and are comfortable. Beyond that, I don't really care what people think. I change the things about my appearance that matter to me, not what others think I should do.
>
> This was not always true. When I was younger, I spent too much time, worry, money, and effort trying to look the way I thought others thought I should look. I was more concerned about what was fashionable or trendy than I should have been. And what do I have to show for it now? Pictures of me in ugly hairstyles and clothes.

My recommendation is that if you are not happy with your appearance, focus on why. Is it because of what you truly believe, or is it because of what you think others believe? If it is because of what you believe, and you want to change, first focus on health. As you become healthier, you will look better.

Depending upon your profession or job, however, what others think may have an impact on your professional future. That is something to take into consideration as well. If everyone else is wearing a suit, wearing sweats and flip flops won't advance your career.

▪ TIME

We cannot change the amount of time we have in a day, week, or year. We can, however, change how we spend our time.

My father was always fond of saying that in a year, five years, ten years, or more, the only certainty was that we would be that much older. Everything else would depend on what we did with that time.

If you want to make changes in your life, take a close look at how you spend your time. Is watching television getting you where you want to go in life? Is going out every night helping you to achieve your goals? Is there any benefit to playing video games? How much time throughout the day are you spending on social media? We all need a certain amount of relaxation. However, like everything else, there needs to be balance, and we need to prioritize.

Five years from now, do you want to have a degree? Do you want a better job? Do you want to make more money? Do you want to have more meaningful relationships? If the answer is "yes" to any of these questions, then you must prioritize your time so that you can achieve these goals. It may involve large time commitments and sacrifices now, but isn't it better than waiting? The sooner you achieve any of these things, the longer you can enjoy them.

If you want changes in your life, it is likely that you will need to make changes in how you spend your time. If you do not want to give up any of your current free time, that is your choice. Keep in mind, however, that your life is probably not going to change from what it is now.

■ FINANCES

Most people I know, myself included, would like to change their financial situation. That is, they would like to improve it. (I have never met anyone who says they have too much money. Maybe I am hanging out in the wrong crowd. Or maybe, no matter how much someone has, there is more they want to do. And "more" might not be for themselves, but for others.)

Unlike some people, I do not think having money is wrong. Money is necessary to buy those items that we must have to survive and that we cannot produce ourselves. Our society is a long way from an agrarian society where people grew their own food, made their own clothing, and built their own shelter. Most people do not raise their own animals for meat and milk or have a garden for fruits and vegetables, never mind growing and grinding their own grain. We need to earn money to buy these and other necessities.

Money is also necessary to buy all those things that make life more enjoyable. There are many luxuries that only money can buy that add to our comfort and enjoyment.

Unfortunately, many people confuse necessities with luxuries.

If you want more money to spend on something, there are two ways to get that money. One is to earn more money. The other is to spend less money on other items and divert that money to the items you want. Let's talk about the second one first.

One way to gain the money to change many situations (buying a house, car, vacation, or other large-ticket item) is to spend less money on luxuries. As I mentioned before, many people confuse necessities and luxuries.

Shoes are a necessity. We cannot go to work or other public places without shoes. Brand-name shoes are a luxury. Yet how many people do you know who spend extra money just because of the logo on the shoe? How many people buy brand-name shoes for their children, even though they outgrow them quickly? Sometimes a certain brand is beneficial related to health or safety. That is different from spending more money just for the logo. Logos cost money.

Clothes are a necessity. Any of us would get into a great deal of trouble if we walked around naked in public. (This does not really apply to the material, but it is funny. I have a recurring dream that I am naked in public. The oddest part? No one notices.) Again, though, brand-name clothes are a luxury. Clothes need to be clean, neat, in good repair, fit well, and, in the case of work, look professional. If we are buying clothes for the label alone, that is a luxury. Labels cost money.

Food is a necessity. The more processed the food is, the more of a luxury it is and the more it costs. Believe it or not, it is possible to take raw ingredients and make a meal. It's called cooking. I do not mean to offend anyone. I know how to cook; I just do not like to cook. I especially do not like to clean up the mess afterwards. I understand those of you who like using highly-processed convenience food. Still, the more processed an item, the more of a luxury it is. If you want to save money, cooking more from scratch and using fewer convenience foods will do this. So will eating out less.

I do not particularly like coffee, but many people do. I can accept that for many people, coffee is a necessity. However, coffee from many coffee houses is a luxury. If you do not agree, I challenge you to track how much you spend each day and multiple it by 365. That is how much you are spending on "trendy" coffee each year. Is it worth it? Or could that money be used better elsewhere?

Another luxury is entertainment. How much do you spend on cable or satellite TV? Is it necessary to have the package that you do? How much do you spend on going out to eat, to movies, and other entertainment? How much do you spend on alcohol and tobacco?

What do you spend on health and beauty products? On getting your hair cut/colored? Are there less-expensive options that you could use? Do you spend money every week on your nails? Is it necessary that you do that?

If you really want to see if there are areas where you could cut back, track all your expenses for one month. And I mean every expense. Carry a notebook (paper or electronic) with you and record every time you buy something. When you buy gas, record not only what you paid for the gas but also anything you bought in the store, even if it was just a snack. Record what you spend whenever you go through the drive-through for a beverage or snack. Record what you spend for lunch. Record what you purchase from the vending machines at work. Record what you buy for your children. Of course, record when you go grocery shopping, clothes shopping, shopping for household products, and everything else. Record everything.

When you get home, or at least on the weekend, enter these amounts into a spreadsheet. Group them into categories that make sense to you. For example, you might want to use food, supplies, entertainment, gas, car expenses, personal expenses, and clothing. Include any weekly expenses that you might have, such as day care or children's allowances. At the end of the month, enter your monthly expenses such as mortgage/rent, utilities, car payments, insurance, etc.

I know it is a pain to gather this much information for a month. The more accurate the information, however, the better decisions you can make regarding changes you want to make. If tracking this amount of detail for a month is too much, at least do it very accurately for a week, multiple it by four, and use that as a monthly total. Then add in your monthly expenses.

Now total the categories. Are you shocked at how much money you spend on some of these categories? Multiply by 12 and see what an average for the year is. Are you shocked even more? Most people are. What else could you have done with that money? Just for fun, multiple it by 10 to see the impact over a decade.

The next step is to use this information to create a budget. Look at which items are luxuries that you could do without. If you are not sure which are luxuries, ask if your parents had them. Did they do without them? If so, are you willing to do without them? Decide what you can eliminate or decrease.

Take a look at the necessities, things like your mortgage/rent, utilities, and transportation costs. Are there ways to decrease these costs? Can you bundle some utilities to save money? Can you adjust the thermostat or turn lights off when no one is in the room? Do you need both a landline and a cell phone?

The purpose of a budget, of course, is to plan in advance how much money you can afford to spend in each category. When you plan a budget, do not forget to include how much you need to save each month for retirement, college (for your children, yourself, or your spouse), vacations (if you want vacations), emergencies (a new furnace, tires, medical expenses not covered by insurance), and other big items such as a down payment for a house or a different car. There are many resources to help you plan a budget. A good place to start is your bank.

If you want to change your financial situation so that you have more money to spend on something you want, or to save for something you will want such as retirement or a college education for your children, one option is to stop spending as much money as you currently do, especially on luxuries.

> Life is a matter of balance. Finances are also a matter of balance. As an example, let me tell you how I try to balance necessities with luxuries. Keep in mind that there is not any right or wrong. This is what works for me, and perhaps you can gain ideas from it.
>
> When I was starting my career and made much less money, I bought cheap shoes. They were all I could afford. I tried to find shoes that looked as professional as possible and were as

comfortable as possible, but they were cheap. And because I spent a great deal of my time walking, my feet were sore most of the time. As I earned more money, I started buying more expensive shoes, mostly so that they would be more comfortable and my feet would not hurt as much. Today, I usually buy a couple of brands that I like in terms of appearance and comfort. I buy these brands not because of the name, but because of their comfort, appearance, and consistent quality. I could buy even more expensive shoes, but to me that would not make sense. Why should I pay more for just a name when the brands I have provide everything I want?

I did not have much money for clothes, either, when I was starting my career. I shopped sales much more than I do now. I paid more attention to buying clothes that I could mix and match to at least give the illusion that I had a larger wardrobe than I did. I even made some of my clothes. Today, there are a few brands that make up most of my wardrobe. I buy these brands because I like the quality and how they fit. Also, I like how easy it is to coordinate them. Clothes impact the impression we make. There are times when that is important to me. When I am writing and no one sees me except the cats, however, I wear old hiking clothes.

One point I want to make is that as our financial situation improves, we have more money for luxuries. However, our financial situation will never improve if we do not take responsibility and live within our current income and/or increase our income.

■ ■ ■

I have a friend who saved a great deal of money over the years by shopping at Goodwill for clothes for herself and her family. They always looked great. The money she saved on clothes was money that she and her husband could use for other items.

■ ■ ■

Another method to control spending is to restrict impulse buying. One way to do this is to wait 24 hours before making a purchase. Another is to create a shopping list before leaving home. If it's not on the list, don't buy it.

■ ■ ■

It is not necessary to give up luxuries, even high-ticket items, if they are important to us, if we balance our purchases. I have a friend who has a passion for a certain, expensive, brand of purse. She has purchased a few over the years. Each time she has, however, she has met at least two out of three criteria: the item was on sale, she had a coupon, and/or she was able to utilize an employee discount.

I have seen this woman choose not to purchase a $5.00 shirt because it was not exactly what she wanted. She is frugal. She manages to get what she wants while staying within her budget. The result is that she and her family have a great house in a nice neighborhood, reliable cars, and a comfortable lifestyle.

■ ■ ■

An important point to remember is that luxuries are things that we do not need; they might not be expensive. Junk is also a luxury. I know a woman who spends money just to spend money. It must make her feel good, because she certainly does not need the majority of items that she buys. Her children certainly do not need all the things she buys for them, either. In fact, it would be much better for them if rather than spend money on "junk" she put the money into a college fund for them. Perhaps the worst part is that she is teaching her children, by example, poor financial habits.

A very important question to ask yourself before buying something is: Why? You may need to keep asking yourself why until you reach the real reason. If the real reason is that you want to impress others or you want them to like you, is that good? Another important question to ask yourself before you spend money is whether this is the best use of your money to accomplish your goals. In other words, practice mindful spending.

Perhaps you decide that you would rather keep your life as it is than to make changes. Perhaps you do not want to make any sacrifices in how you spend your money. That is fine if you can pay your bills. But then accept that that is why you do not have some of the things you want. It is a matter of prioritizing.

The alternative to spending less money, of course, is to earn more money. At the very least, do everything you need to do to earn a raise or bonus whenever it is available. Also, do everything you need to do to obtain the maximum amount of increase in your wage or salary. In some situations, it really is not that hard. You just have to work harder and better than your co-workers. Keep in mind that your employer is paying you for what you do now. If you want to earn more, you need to do and contribute more.

A faster way to earn more money is to work for a promotion. Gain the skills and knowledge necessary to advance. This will probably provide a bigger increase than any single raise, and each raise after that will be more because it will be based on a larger base salary. Discuss with your supervisor what promotions are possible and what you need to do to achieve them.

Another option is to gain the skills and knowledge necessary to move to another company. Sometimes this is the best way to advance. Your current company may not be able to pay more. There are many economic issues involved. If it is a small company, there might not be any opportunities for advancement. Or perhaps management at your current company is taking you for granted and you need to move to another company where you will be appreciated and rewarded.

Sometimes you can earn additional income through part-time or temporary work. Many places hire over the holidays, for example. Depending upon your skills, you might be able to do side work in your home. Many entrepreneurs and solopreneurs need outside help to run their businesses. Assisting them could even lead to your own business.

Much of my professional and financial success came from working for the next rung in the corporate ladder (when I worked for a corporation). When I finished college and my internship, I had multiple job opportunities. I took the one with the most opportunities for advancement. No matter what level I was at, I was working to achieve the next level.

■ ■ ■

I have two friends that I admire greatly. One quit college to marry and have children. Although she always had a job, she was never able to advance very far without her college degree. When her husband decided he wanted a divorce, it was a wake-up call for her. She went back to college and finished her degree, while working full-time. This enabled her to obtain promotions that had been closed to her before.

Another friend, a single mom, was raising two daughters without help from their father. She finally decided she did not want to continue the way she was. She went to college and obtained a bachelor's degree. When she finished, she went back and obtained her MBA. She did all this while working full-time. Not only did she greatly improve her career and financial situation; she was also a great role model for her daughters, both of whom went to college after high school.

Of course, you might decide that you do not want to work harder or take on more responsibility. You might not want to spend even more time away from your family. You might not want to deal with the extra stress. You might not want to make the sacrifices that are required. That is fine, but then accept that this is why you do not have some of the things that you want. As with deciding what to spend your money on, it is a matter of prioritization.

These are all options for changing your financial situation. If you choose not to change, then accept that you are where you are because of the choices you have made. We will discuss accepting situations in the next chapter.

▪ RELATIONSHIPS

Professional and personal relationships are an integral part of our lives. It is important to our welfare that our relationships support us and are good for us. Those that are not need to be addressed. Unless the situation is extremely bad, trying to change it is a good first step.

It is extremely important to remember, though, that you cannot change anyone else, just as no one can change you. Change is an individual decision. You can create an environment to encourage change in someone, but you cannot change him or her.

One way to change your professional environment to encourage change in others is by communicating. Tell your employer what you want related to your job and ask what you need to do to get it. Tell your employees what you expect from them and what they can expect from you in return. Tell your suppliers, associates, and others in your professional life what you need from them, what you expect from them, what your standards are. If you do not, they will never know. Telepathy only exists in science fiction and fantasy.

The same applies to your personal relationships. Tell your partner, parents, children, friends, neighbors, and others in your life what you want and need from them. Tell them what you think and feel. Tell them how their words and actions affect you. If you do not tell them, they will not know. Of course, respectful communication is critical in creating and maintaining a positive relationship.

Another way to change your professional and/or personal environment to encourage change in others is to change your behavior toward them. If you treat the other person differently, he or she might treat you differently. People often respond to whatever treatment we give them. This might mean treating them with more respect, or it might mean standing up to them and being assertive.

To gain ideas on which behaviors to change, think about the situation from the other person's point of view. Would you want to be involved in a relationship (as an employee, employer, customer, spouse, parent, etc.) with you? Why or why not? Does this give you any ideas for changing yourself to change the environment to encourage the other person to change?

- **LIFESTYLE**

Lifestyle incorporates so many things. Where you live (country, region, city, suburbs, rural). What you live in (apartment, condo, small house, large house). How you spend your money (necessities, luxuries, charity, travel, family). The level of your community involvement. Your social life, interests, hobbies. Your profession or career. Your lifestyle is how you live your life.

If there is anything about your lifestyle that you want to change, you probably can. It will likely take hard work, dedication, and sacrifice, but you can probably do it.

Before you decide to make changes, however, determine why you want to make those changes. Is it because it is important to you, or is it because you think it should be important? Do you want to make changes because it is right for you (and your partner/family if you have one) or because you want to impress others?

I grew up on a dairy farm. Although I have lived in small cities and towns, I really prefer the country. I like the privacy and solitude. I like to be surrounded by nature. Even though my husband was raised in the city, he, too, likes country life. When we moved back to Wisconsin and were looking for a place to live, we looked first for a place in the country. Although we found land we liked, it did not contain houses that we liked. Although we found houses we liked, they were on small lots of land, and we wanted acres. When we found land we liked, but without a house, we decided to build.

We built the house we wanted. It is large, open, with many big windows. We wanted to bring the outside inside. We built what was right for us. We did not build it to impress others. We built it for us to enjoy. Too many people we know have bought or built to impress others and are not happy with what they have or have spent more than they could afford.

■ INTERNAL FACTORS

Remember, external factors are outside of us and internal factors are inside of us. Examples of internal factors include our thoughts, beliefs, values, personality traits, behavioral choices, emotional issues, and personal history.

What are your internal factors related to health, appearance, time, finances, relationships, and lifestyle? What is in your personal history related to these things? What emotional issues or ties do you have to these? What have your behavior choices been in the past related to these? What are your personality traits related to these items? What are your values related to these? How do they shape your beliefs about these items? How do your beliefs shape your thoughts? (These are also excellent questions to ask about professional and personal situations.)

Why do you believe what you do about each of these situations? Are these beliefs helping you move forward, or are they holding you back? Are there any internal factors you need to address to change any of the situations discussed?

To give you an idea of internal factors, here are a few of mine that have an impact on my overall wellness.

> One of my core values is responsibility. Even as a child I was extremely responsible. I believe that I am responsible for all aspects of my life. I am responsible to do what needs to be done to become the person I want and to have the life I want. My actions continue to reinforce this because the more responsibility I take for myself, the more I achieve what I want. A drawback to this is that I tend to take on responsibility that is not mine, and that has affected some of my relationships. (Oddly enough, some people sometimes think I'm

controlling—go figure.) It has been difficult to adopt the philosophy of "not my circus, not my monkeys," but it has been worth it.

■ ■ ■

My father emphasized the importance of formal and informal education as I was growing up. Probably largely because of this, I highly value learning in general. When we learn something new, it changes who we are. I like that. I like that I am constantly changing and growing. It makes it easier to change as necessary. The results of my learning reinforce its importance.

■ ■ ■

I am a registered dietitian by background. Much of my college education was science-based. It affects how I view and interpret information, especially information in the media. I'm skeptical of much of what I read. A benefit to this is that I can make better health choices than many people. A drawback is that I find it difficult to deal with people who jump from one health fad to another without acknowledging scientific data. This has affected some relationships.

I am sure you have heard the phrase, "There is no reality, only perception." This is true. Our perception of the world becomes our reality. This is also true as it relates to ourselves. One's perception of oneself becomes one's reality.

If you want to change anything in your life, start by looking at your perception of yourself. Is it accurate? There are some people who do not give themselves enough credit. They do not think they are that good or that worthy. There are others who create a perception about themselves that is much better than what others have of them. They might do this to make themselves feel good about themselves, to justify past actions, or to avoid looking too closely at who they really are. And then there are those who have an accurate perception of themselves. They see their faults and work to overcome them rather than let their faults define who they are. They see their strengths and accomplishments and take credit for their hard work and persistence.

When it comes down to it, if we want to change any aspect of our life, we, ourselves, have to change. Usually, if we want to change, we need to change our beliefs. Then we can change our thoughts. Then we can change our actions.

Simply stated, if we believe we cannot do something, we will not do it until we change to believe that we can do it. Or until we at least change our belief that we can try. When we try, and succeed, we gain confidence. If we don't succeed, we can still gain confidence because we know, if nothing else, we survived. If we survived one attempt, we can survive a second. Also, if we try and don't succeed we learn what didn't work and we can try something different.

Summary

If you are not satisfied with an aspect of your life, a good place to start is to determine why. Once you know what is causing your dissatisfaction, then you can determine what to change.

One technique that you can use is to describe, in as much detail as you can, what your ideal life would be like. Compare this with what you have. What needs to be changed? If there is more than one item, what is the most important to change?

From that point, determine how to change it. The first step might be as simple as talking to the appropriate person.

Tell him or her what you want and ask what you need to do to achieve it. Expecting others to know what you want without your telling them is not realistic. Neither is it realistic to expect others to give you what you want just because you want it. However, if you are willing to change, they might be, too.

Consider any internal factors related to how you perceive change. Do you like change? Do you fear change? Are you uncomfortable with it, but, if necessary, you'll make one anyway? Are there any internal changes that you want to make?

Have you noticed that if you are to change anything in your life, it comes down to changing you? And this is very, very good. You, and only you, have the power to change you. Because you have this power, this control, over your life, you can make your life what you want it to be.

You have the power and control to at least try to change things. Often, once you try, you will succeed. You will never succeed if you never try.

There is another important point I want to make. If you are in a committed relationship, you must work with your partner. The two of you must choose together the life you want and how to make it happen. For example, you cannot decide unilaterally that you are too stressed, quit your job, and expect your partner to pay the bills alone. Even something like going back to college must be a joint decision because it will also affect your partner.

Exercises

The following exercises are designed to help you decide if you want to try to change a situation. You can use these same exercises for as many situations as you want.

- **EXERCISE 2.1:** Pick a situation that you listed in Chapter 1. It does not matter which one, but you might want to pick the one that is bothering you the most or that would have the greatest impact on your life if it changed. Describe it in as much detail as possible. Describing it in detail might help you to recognize all the internal and external factors involved. Another step that can help you is to pick two colors of highlighters. Use one color to highlight the external factors and the other to highlight internal factors.

- **EXERCISE 2.2:** Describe in as much detail as possible your desired result. What outcome do you want by changing the situation? The more specific you can be, the more likely you are to achieve a satisfying result. For example, remember the story of my friend who had someone take his position? If his desired result had simply been to keep a job, any job, he would have had a job doing all the work and the person who took his position would have taken all the credit. My friend would have been miserable. Instead, he created a proposal for a new position that was also his ideal job. His supervisor accepted the proposal, and my friend achieved a better position than he had before.

- **EXERCISES 2.3–2.6:** These exercises go beyond the simple advantages/disadvantages exercise. Although looking at advantages to changing and disadvantages to not changing is good, it doesn't reveal the hidden payoffs to staying the same. If these hidden payoffs are not recognized, it can sabotage decision-making. For example, on the surface it might look like the best thing to do is to change jobs. However, it is not likely that everything about your current job is horrible. There are probably things that you like, maybe certain co-workers, that you will miss if you leave. By identifying and addressing these hidden payoffs to not changing early, you can better cope with any losses or stress that change might bring.

By going through these exercises in order you can first catch the hidden payoffs that might sabotage your decision-making later. Then you can identify what you are giving up or what the costs are of not changing. Once you go through this thought process it is easier to accept advantages of changing and disadvantages of not changing without the hidden payoffs lurking in the background, potentially sabotaging your efforts to change.

Some of your answers for the exercises might be similar, or even the same. That is fine. This is more about the thought process and what you discover than it is putting the "right" answer in the "right" box.

- **EXERCISE 2.7:** Review all the information you have written and decide if you want to change. If you decide to change, continue to the next exercise. If the costs of changing are too high and you decide not to change, consider accepting the situation instead.

    Something to consider is that it may not be feasible to change now, but can you develop and implement a plan so that you can make a change in six months, a year, five years? If so, in the next chapter determine how to accept the situation temporarily.

- **EXERCISE 2.8:** Determine the steps you need to take to change the situation. Consider both external and internal factors related to the situation (refer to your highlighted items). This can help you determine the external and internal steps you need to take. For example, an external step you might need to take to change your work situation is to talk to your supervisor. An internal step that you might need to take is to overcome your fear of conflict. It can also be beneficial to add a timeframe indicating when you will complete each step.

Exercise 2-1
What situation do I want to address?

Pick one of the situations you listed in the tables in Chapter 1. Describe it here in as much detail as possible, explaining why you are not satisfied. After you are done, highlight the external and internal factors to reference later.

Exercise 2-2
What is my desired result?

For the situation you identified, describe in detail your desired result.

Exercise 2-3
If I choose to do nothing, what do I gain?

For the situation you identified, describe in detail what you will gain if you do nothing.

Exercise 2-4
If I choose to change, what do I lose?

For the situation you identified, describe in detail what you will lose if you change the situation.

Exercise 2-5
If I choose to change, what do I gain?

For the situation you identified, describe in detail what you will gain if you change the situation.

2 CHANGE IT · ACCEPT IT · LEAVE IT

Exercise 2-6
If I choose to do nothing, what do I lose?

For the situation you identified, describe in detail what you will lose if you do nothing.

Exercise 2-7
Do I want to change the situation?

Review all the information you have written. Do you want to try to change the situation? Why or why not? Write your reasons here. Remember that you can try to change the situation as many times as you want. Also, at any point you can decide to try accepting it or leaving it instead.

Exercise 2-8
What steps do I need to take to change the situation?

If you decide to change the situation, list the steps that you need to take to change it. Consider both the external and internal factors you identified in Exercise 2.1. You also might want to add a timeframe.

Accept It 3

IN MANY, PERHAPS most, situations the best choice is to accept it. A few general examples follow.

Anything in the past must be accepted. We cannot go back in time and change it. We cannot leave our past. It is there, it is part of us. The best we can do is to accept it, try to fix things if we can, and move on. (If there are extremely bad things in your past, you might want to seek professional help to come to terms with them. Seeking help is a positive action.) Complaining, whining, and using the past as an excuse for the present do not change anything or solve anything. All you accomplish when you do this is give your past even more power and control over you.

Perfection does not exist. No one will ever be perfect. No situation will ever be perfect. If you are waiting for a person or situation to be perfect, it is not going to happen. However, we can strive for excellence. Excellence can change from day-to-day and year-to-year. Striving for excellence leaves room for error and changes. In determining which choice (change, accept, leave) is best for you, decide what would be an excellent outcome and work for that.

Sometimes we need to accept that what is right for us is not what family, friends, or society think is right for us. We need to accept that we will not meet their expectations and that it does not matter if we do not, as long as we do not harm others. Disappointing others is not harming them. If we are living our lives responsibly, and they don't like it, that is their problem.

There are also many situations that are just not that important; accept them and move on rather than spend any more time and energy on them than necessary. For example, there are probably people in your life (I know that there are in mine) that have personality quirks that annoy you. It's not that they are doing anything wrong, you just don't like it.

> I like quiet. I know people who are loud. They talk loudly, laugh loudly, and walk loudly. I have decided to accept that that is who they are. I could address it with them, but all it would do is cause hard feelings. If I had a work cubicle next to them, and their loudness affected my work, then that would be a different situation and I would need to work to change it. But for people that I see occasionally? Accepting them as they are is the easiest and best choice. And who knows? Maybe my quietness bothers them.

There are times when it is best to accept the situation and then determine how to manage it. Managing the situation is largely determining how we are going to react to the situation so that it has the minimal negative impact on us. An example is the weather. We can't control whether it rains, snows, sleets, or anything else. All we can do is accept that it is what it is and decide how we are going to manage it. Maybe we move an outdoor activity inside or reschedule it. Maybe we leave for work early if the weather will make the roads bad or traffic slow. Becoming angry isn't a good choice. It just makes a difficult situation more difficult.

The remainder of this chapter follows the same format as the previous chapter. It provides different ideas on when it might be better to accept certain aspects of situations. Again, it is not meant to be a comprehensive list. Use it as a method to think about what is important to you.

Professional Situations
- **PROFESSION/INDUSTRY**

There are some things about certain professions and industries that we simply need to accept. Some require specific degrees, registration, licenses, and/or other requirements. Some do not pay that well. Some do not have many openings. Some do not have much opportunity for growth or advancement. Some require extensive travel and/or relocation. Some require high levels of dedication and determination to succeed. I am sure you can think of more examples that apply to your profession.

These are things that should be considered before making a career choice. If, however, we made the career choice first and then found out about these things, we need to accept that we made a decision without all the facts and decide what we are going to do.

Once we accept the things about a profession or industry that we cannot change, then we can determine what we want to do. It might be possible to make changes in a situation. It might be possible to accept that, although not ideal, there are enough positives to make it worthwhile to stay in that profession. Or it might be necessary to accept something until we can leave for a new profession.

When I was in college to become a dietitian, an assignment for one class was to interview someone in a position that we would like to obtain someday. At the time, I wanted to become the director of a hospital foodservice department. I contacted the director of a large hospital in a nearby city and he agreed to meet with me.

During our conversation, he said that although dietitians were good for clinical roles, he would never hire a dietitian for a foodservice management role because dietitians did not know anything about business. I have since learned that many healthcare administrators believe the same. Possibly the primary reason is that most dietitians prefer clinical roles and do not want foodservice management roles. Those who take management roles, even though they do not want them, are probably not that successful, which adds to the belief that dietitians aren't good at it.

I have had to accept that this is a common perception about dietitians. However, that did not mean that I had to accept that this belief applied to me. The main reason I did not want potential employers to believe this about me was because I liked the management aspect better than the clinical. The college I attended offered a double major, bachelor of science degrees in dietetics and foodservice administration. I took it. By adding one class, I also obtained a business minor. I chose an internship that offered both clinical and foodservice management rotations.

The business aspect of my education netted me three job offers after my internship was complete. The quality of my work enabled me to advance at the company I chose.

I offer this as an example that although we might have to accept something about our profession, that does not mean that we cannot be the exception.

- **POSITION/JOB RESPONSIBILITIES**

I doubt that anyone has a position that they love every minute of every day. I think everyone has at least a few things that they don't like about their jobs. Remember, nothing is perfect. If it is not possible to change it, is it possible to accept it? The exercises at the end of the chapter can help you decide.

There is also the possibility that the situation is acceptable at present but you know it will not be acceptable to you in the future.

In college, I worked as a dietary aide and cook in hospitals, as a waitress, and in various other foodservice positions. All were acceptable as a way to earn money to put myself through college and to gain foodservice experience. None would have been acceptable long-term. That was why I was going to college, after all. In each position (I always had 2-3 jobs at any one time) I focused on what I liked about the position and the fact that it was temporary. I decided early that I could survive anything, as long as it was temporary.

Even after I finished college and my dietetic internship, the first position I had, as a foodservice director in a nursing home for a national long-term care company, was acceptable only as a stepping stone for promotions to positions that I did want. The work and demands for the director position were acceptable to me at the time because it was temporary and because that was what I had to do to advance. It would not have been acceptable as a life-long career.

It seems that many people today expect to have their ideal job immediately. It doesn't work like that. You need to gain the knowledge and experience necessary to succeed. I owe my success at every level to what I had learned at the previous level.

- **COMPANY/EMPLOYER**

No company is perfect for everyone. What is important to some people may not be important to others. What matters is how good of a fit the company is for you. If the overall fit is good, it might be possible to accept those few things that are not ideal.

When I finished my internship, I had three good options for employment. I chose the largest company because it offered the greatest opportunity for advancement. That was what was most important to me at the time. One of the companies had no opportunity for advancement because it was so small. The other was large, but the turnover was so low that I could have waited for years before any position opened. The position I took did not pay as much as the other positions, but I knew that with promotions I would soon be making more than I could ever have with the other two. I wanted promotions not only for the higher long-term income but also for the increased variety and challenge. The company I chose was the best fit for me. For others, one of the other companies might have been the best fit.

If there is something you don't like about your company/employer, take a close look at whether it is really the company or if it is the industry or profession. If it is the nature of the profession, moving to another company might not change anything. The nature of the business might force all companies to act in similar ways. Then it becomes a matter of deciding if you want to accept it or move to another profession.

- **INTERNAL FACTORS**

External factors are outside of us. Many professional-life external factors have been discussed, although you can probably think of more that pertain to your life. Internal factors are inside of us. Our internal factors can make it difficult to accept situations, even when accepting it might be the best choice.

If you are having trouble accepting a situation, evaluate which internal factors might be involved. Is it stubbornness? Pride? Ego? A need to always be right? A fear to admit failure or defeat? Have you invested too much to accept that you made a mistake? What is keeping you from accepting a situation when that might be the best choice?

Conversely, there may be internal factors that encourage you to accept a situation when changing or leaving might be better. What do you truly believe about your abilities and skills related to your profession or position? Are you dissatisfied but do not think you could get anything better when maybe you could? Have you looked?

Before deciding to accept a professional situation, or before deciding to reject the possibility of accepting a situation, consider your internal factors.

Personal Situations
- **RELATIONSHIP STATUS**

There is so much pressure in our society to be in a relationship that it's scary. And it starts at a very young age.

> I know a woman who has been asking and teasing her daughter about boyfriends since the child was two years old. The unspoken message, for more than a decade now, is that the girl needs to have a boyfriend. At 12, she has one. The boy may turn out to be abusive (physically, mentally, or emotionally), but she has a boyfriend because that is what she was raised to believe that she must have. I hate to think how much of her self-image is tied to being a girlfriend as compared to being tied to who she is as a person.

In the previous chapter I emphasized asking yourself why you want a particular relationship before trying to change your status. What I would like to do here is to encourage you to accept your relationship status (whatever it is), focus on the positive aspects, and enjoy it. (Unless you are in an abusive relationship. Then you need to take action, which may include seeking professional help.) There is so much emphasis on being in a relationship that sometimes I think we get caught up in the destination and forget to enjoy the journey.

Another aspect of relationships is that not only does he or

she need to be the right one for you, you need to be the right one for him or her, and it needs to be the right time for both of you. Sometimes we cannot change any of these three. Then the best thing to do might be to accept it and move on.

■ PARENTHOOD (OR NOT)

One aspect of parenthood may be wanting children and needing to accept that you cannot have children the usual way. Accepting this enables you to look at other methods of becoming a parent such as in vitro fertilization, a surrogate mother, adoption, or becoming a foster parent. If none of these is an option, then the need is to accept that you will not be a parent. That does not mean, however, that you cannot be involved in lives of children through other means such as being an aunt or volunteering.

Another aspect is non-parenthood. Not wanting to have children or not wanting to be a parent can be very difficult for family, friends, and society to accept. What we need to do is to do what is right for us and accept that others may not accept our decision. That is their problem, not ours.

> I never wanted children. I never wanted to be a parent. I remember as a young child getting a baby doll from my grandma. It was one of the first ones that you could feed a bottle of water to and in a little while it would "wet" its diaper. I dressed it, fed it a bottle, pretended to feed it food, changed the diaper, changed the other clothes because they were wet, and put the doll to bed. I remember thinking, "That was boring!" Yet I could play with other toys for hours. Another telling point was that all my stuffed animals had names and personalities. That poor little doll never even had a gender, let alone a name.

> I hoped that my brothers would have children, because I thought being an aunt would be really cool. (It is.) I also thought being a grandma would be fun, as long as I did not have to go through the mother step first. That worked, too, because it just happened that my husband had children who were almost grown when we married. And being a grandma is fun. And I am still glad I did not go through the mother step.

When we are certain about what we want, or do not want, it is important that we stick to that even if family, friends, and society think that they know what is best for us. We need to accept that we, not others, know what is best for us.

Another aspect of parenthood is determining what you can and should change with your children and what you need to accept. This is an extreme example, but if your child is a spoiled brat, disrespectful to others, irresponsible, lies, and is involved in illegal activities, you, as her parent, are responsible for trying to change her behavior. A major part of parenting is raising responsible children.

If, however, you like music and your child likes sports, accept that her interests and yours are not the same. You can introduce her to everything you like, but accept that she is her own person and not a mini-you.

In the previous chapter I mentioned that you might want to change or improve the relationship you have with your children. That is good, but again remember that you may need to accept that your child may want a different relationship than you do. This may be especially true as your child grows to adulthood.

▪ INTERESTS

Interests are those things that we do for fun, to add something extra to our lives, to make us feel good. We don't have to be good at them, and it's fine to accept that we are not.

I've played golf for some time now. At first, I tried competing with my husband and his sons. I was consistently frustrated because I did not hit the ball as far as they did. At the time, I did not want to accept certain facts. I'm much shorter than they are, my arms are shorter than theirs, I don't have the muscle mass they do, and I don't have the upper-body strength they do. Once I accepted these facts, and the resultant conclusion that I was never going to hit it as far as they did unless I devoted my life to learning how to overcome these physical realities, I started to enjoy the game more. Now I compete with myself. As long as I continue to improve, I'm satisfied.

Since our interests are generally for fun, it can be easy to accept situations related to them because the cost is generally low.

My husband and I like to eat out. We also like to try new places. Whenever we try something new, we run the risk that the food and/or service might be bad. It's an easy risk to take, and easy to accept if it is, because the cost is low and we have the chance of finding our new favorite restaurant.

Sometimes accepting aspects of our interests is more difficult. Sometimes things cannot be changed, and we need to decide whether to accept it or leave it.

I foster mother cats and their kittens for the local humane society. I thoroughly enjoy the work and the knowledge that I have helped these cats. The difficult part is giving them back to the humane society for adoption. Part of me wants to keep them all, but I know that it is not realistic to adopt every cat I foster. Three cats of my own are more than enough. (My husband might argue that it is one or two too many.) What I choose to focus on is that because of what I have done for the fosterlings, they will be able to find homes, and better homes, than if they had not been fostered. I accept that I will need to give them back.

- **INTERNAL FACTORS**

The same internal factors discussed under the professional situation section can also apply here. If you are hesitant to accept a situation, or have difficulty accepting situations in general, ask yourself, "Why?" Continue asking yourself this until you have a list of reasons and until you think you have gotten to the bottom of the list.

Also, try to determine where your beliefs originated. Do they make sense for who you are today? Do they make sense for the world today?

Overall Wellness
- **HEALTH**

Although I think it is important that we all make the changes necessary to maintain as high a level of health as possible, there are some things that most of us need to accept.

Ignoring a disease or health condition will not make it go away. Accepting that you have that condition and taking the prescribed treatment to manage that condition is imperative. For example, if someone has diabetes, it is important that she follow her physician's orders for medication/insulin, diet, and exercise.

If you choose not to make the changes necessary to be as healthy as possible, then accept the consequences of your decision. It's better to accept them than to complain about them. Complaining doesn't change anything.

■ APPEARANCE

There are some aspects of our appearance that we need to accept. We will never be taller than what we are. We can give the illusion of being taller by wearing high heels, but we will never actually be taller. We cannot change our skeletal structure. If we have a large body frame, we will not be able to change that into a small body frame.

In addition to accepting aspects of our appearance that we cannot change, I think it is good to embrace the aspects that we cannot change.

Like most women, I have spent a good portion of my life not liking my body.

My breasts are too small. My butt is too big. My hips are too wide. My thighs are too heavy. My stomach sticks out. The only thing that I have consistently liked about my body shape is that I have a defined waist.

I don't remember how old I was, maybe in my forties, when I first saw a picture of "The Birth of Venus" by Botticelli. You have probably seen a picture of this painting as well. Venus, the Roman goddess of love and beauty, is standing, naked, on a seashell near the shore.

I do not remember where I was when I saw this picture, or what I was doing, but I do remember vividly what I was thinking.

"Huh. Small breasts. Wide hips. Heavy thighs. Can't see her butt, but I'd bet it's big. Stomach sticks out. She does have a waist, though...

She looks a little like me...

OH. MY. GOSH.

I have the body of a goddess!"

That realization changed how I viewed my body, and the human body in general, forever.

The human body comes in all shapes and sizes. And although I do not have the scientific evidence to support this, I suspect that women's bodies come in even more shapes and sizes than men's do. I also think ours (women's) are more likely to change throughout our lives.

I finally realized and accepted that there are no good body shapes and no bad body shapes. Different cultures at different times try to convince their members that there are, but there aren't. It's all just opinion. I'm sure that there was probably a goddess somewhere, at some time, for every body shape that there is.

What matters is that our bodies are healthy and capable of doing what we want them to do. If they are, then our bodies are just fine, no matter what shape or size they are.

One of the best and most far-reaching decisions I ever made was based on this realization. I decided to focus on my body's health rather than its shape. I can change my health. I can't change my basic body shape.

Besides having a healthier body, I was finally able to view my body more objectively. And guess what? The parts that I thought were too small? They aren't. And the parts I thought were too big? They aren't.

There may also be aspects of our appearance that we could change and decide not to change. It's fine to decide not to color our hair anymore and let it go gray, for example.

The important thing to ask is what is important to you and why. Once you have complete, honest answers it becomes much easier to decide what to accept and what to change.

- **TIME**

The previous chapter discussed how, if we want to change our lives, we will probably need to change how we spend our time. If we choose not to change how we spend our time, then we generally need to accept that our lives will not change. As with everything else, there is not any right or wrong answer to this.

I have a friend who for years has complained about not making more money. For years I have encouraged her to go back to college and finish her degree so she can apply for higher-level jobs. For years she has chosen to spend her time going out and relaxing at home rather than taking classes. She has neither chosen to take the steps necessary to change her situation nor to accept that she is where she is because of this choice. She just complains, which does not help her.

- **FINANCES**

In many ways we live in a materialistic culture. We are constantly bombarded with the idea that we need more, bigger, and better. The important thing is to decide what we truly need (as discussed in the previous chapter) and what we simply want. There is nothing wrong with wanting things. What frequently gets us into trouble, though, is when we don't determine why we want those things.

> I certainly enjoy the finer things in life. Of course, my idea of "finer things" might be different from other people's. I like living in the country. I like owning enough land that people cannot build close to me. I like having privacy, quiet, and solitude when I want it. I like being close to nature. I like to travel and see the world. I like having clothes that fit and look good. I like eating good food and drinking good wine much better than consuming poor-quality food and drink. And cats. I really like having cats. All this takes money, and I am willing to work for it.
>
> I know the lifestyle I want because of who I am and my values. Luckily, my husband wants the same lifestyle (except maybe for the cats). It's about us, not about what others do.

Too many people get caught up in thinking that they must have what everyone else has without thinking about whether it is right for them. They end up spending money they cannot afford on "bigger and more."

Think about what you want and why. Why is extremely important. If you want a bigger house, nicer car, and all the latest electronic gadgets because you truly want these things and it is worth it to you to work extra to get them, that is fine. But do not do it just because that is what everyone else has. Do not do it just to keep up with the neighbors. (For all you know, the neighbors might be facing bankruptcy.) If you are spending money just to impress others, take a close look at why it is important to you to impress others with material possessions.

Something else to think about is that you are constantly teaching your children through your actions. For example, if you buy them everything they want, you are teaching them to expect instant gratification. Is that going to help them as adults? Or would it be better to teach them to work for what they want?

Think about what is most important for you. It might be more important to have more time with your family rather than more money to spend on material items. To do this you might make a conscious decision to work less, make less, and have fewer material items so that you can have more time with your family.

It is fine to accept where you are financially, if you are meeting all your financial obligations. (It is not acceptable to expect other people to make sacrifices so that you can have things that you are not willing to work for yourself.) If you make the decision to accept where you are financially, then truly accept it. Do not complain about what you do not have. Either stop complaining and accept it, or change it.

■ RELATIONSHIPS

Relationships are an area where accepting and then managing a situation can be a good tactic. Often it is not worth leaving the situation and there is not any way to change the situation because there is not any way to change people. Any person can decide that he or she wants to change, but we cannot make them change. We can encourage them to change, we can create an environment to make change easier for them, but only they can decide to change. Sometimes, too, they might like to change but it is not possible or practical.

> As a simple example, my husband snores. It's not a situation that is going to change. I certainly am not going to leave him over something as petty as snoring. So I accept that he snores and manage the situation. Usually all I need to do is fall asleep before he does. He still snores, but I don't hear it. If it's really bad, I can sleep in the guest room.

We all have relatives who refuse to fall off the family tree no matter how much we would like to prune that branch. It probably is not worth it for us to cut all connections with the family because of this person. If trying to change the situation by talking to them does not work, then accept that this is who they are. There may be times, too, when accepting it is better than addressing it and causing a family feud. Accept it and try to manage the situation. Managing might include minimizing the time you spend with them. If nothing else, remember the humorous stories it will create later.

Most of us must work or deal with people who annoy us. Sometimes we can change the situation by talking to the person. If we don't say something, they will not know that it bothers us. If they aren't doing anything illegal or against company policy, however, we may need to accept that that is the way they are and find a way to work with them anyway.

Keep in mind when dealing with people is that there is no "one best way" to do things. Just because someone is not doing something the way we would does not mean that they are wrong. It does not matter how other people are leading their lives if it does not impact us. If it does impact us, then we need to address the issue. If it does not impact us, then accept it and let it go.

An extremely important thing to remember, however, is that we do not need to accept abusive behavior from anyone. If you are in an abusive situation, seek professional help to assist you in changing or leaving the situation.

▪ LIFESTYLE

Many components of lifestyle were mentioned in the previous chapter. There may be things about your lifestyle that you cannot change. More likely, there are results you might like to achieve, but you do not want to make the sacrifices necessary to achieve them. That is fine. Just accept that this is the decision that you made.

For example, would it be worth the sacrifice of taking an additional job to earn the money to take your family to Europe for a bonding experience? Or could you bond just as well with an inexpensive local trip? If so, accept that this is the vacation you can afford and enjoy it.

Perhaps it would be worth the sacrifice of taking another job temporarily because the trip to Europe would include your children meeting distant relatives. In that case, accept that you will have less free time while you earn the money necessary to go, and focus on how it will be worth the effort. Depending upon the age of your children, you can enlist and expect their help. If you are working an extra job to make the trip happen, your children can help by doing more chores at home.

With lifestyle, there are not any right or wrong answers. Take a look at what you want, why you want it, and what you have to do to achieve it. Then decide if it is best for you to change it or accept it.

▪ INTERNAL FACTORS

The information on internal factors discussed throughout the book can be used in any chapter and any section. You might want to go back and reread some of them. The following are some additional considerations.

Sometimes our thoughts and beliefs can get in the way of our accepting others. Just because they do not share our thoughts and beliefs, it does not mean that they are wrong, or that we are wrong. In so many situations, there is no one right way.

If you expect others to respect your thoughts and beliefs, then you need to respect others' thoughts and beliefs, even if they are different from yours. As long as they are not harming you, why does it matter?

If we want others to accept us, then we need to accept others. It only works if it goes both ways.

Something that you might want to consider is if you are accepting a situation, are you accepting by default? Is the choice to accept the situation the best one for you, or are you choosing to accept it because you don't want to change? If so, then is accepting it truly the best choice for you?

Summary

If changing the situation is not possible, or not worth the time and effort to accomplish, accepting the situation might be the best choice. Remember, though, that accepting it means truly accepting it. If you are still complaining about it, you have not accepted it. If it still has power over you, you have not accepted it. If that is the case, you might want to reevaluate changing the situation or consider leaving the situation.

Perception can be a determining factor in our ability to accept a situation. Remember the concept, "There is no reality, only perception." Your perception is your reality. Is it accurate?

Keeping situations in perspective can help us accept them. Maintaining an accurate perception, however, can be difficult, especially if we have strong emotions attached to the situation. We may not be interpreting the situation accurately. Try looking at the situation from the other person's perspective or from an outsider's perspective. Sometimes it can help to ask someone to share his or her perspective with you. This can help determine if we really need to leave or change the situation, or if it makes sense to accept it.

In most situations, if you cannot change it, or it is not worth the effort to change it, ask yourself if you can accept it permanently. If yes, then accept it and manage the situation.

If the answer is no, then ask yourself if you can accept it temporarily. If yes, then develop a plan to enable you to leave the situation at a later date, implement the plan, and stay until you can leave. Until you can leave, focus on how you will be able to leave the situation, not on how much you do not like the situation. That will just hold you back.

If no, you cannot accept it even temporarily, then look for a way to leave the situation as quickly as possible. (Leaving is discussed in the next chapter.)

If you think there might be internal factors that are keeping you from accepting a situation, go back and read the internal factors sections.

> When I was a child my family was poor. Dad was a dairy farmer in Wisconsin. We always had enough to eat because he sold the milk to the local cheese factory and received a very good price on cheese. Mom had a big garden. We ate lots of potatoes. Our clothes were always clean, but not always new.

There were advantages that many people would take for granted that my brothers and I simply did not have. And yet we all put ourselves through college (our parents did not have money to send us), have successful careers, and have better lives than our parents did.

It never occurred to me as a child or young adult that I should be upset about this. It was just the way it was. Once I was old enough to understand that some people would be upset and complain about growing up the way I did, I decided I was not going to do that. I have always accepted that this was my childhood. My parents did the best they could with what they had and what they knew. And since as an adult I am responsible, independent, self-sufficient, successful, and happy, I still don't see that I have anything to complain about.

Exercises

The following exercises are designed to help you decide if you want to try to accept a situation. Remember that accepting the situation means truly accepting it, coming to terms with it, finding peace with it, or whatever term you want to use. Accepting is active. If you continue to complain about it, then you have not accepted it.

- **Exercise 3.1:** If you chose not to try to change the situation you listed in Chapter 2, use it for this exercise. If you decided to try to change it, then pick another situation for this exercise. (Of course, you may evaluate as many situations as you want for changing before moving on to this exercise.) Whichever situation you pick, describe it here in as much detail as possible. You can use the highlighters again to help identify external and internal factors, using a different color for each.

- **Exercise 3.2:** Describe in as much detail as possible your desired result. What outcome do you want by accepting the situation? The more specific you can be, the more likely you are to achieve a satisfying result.

- **Exercises 3.3–3.6:** These exercises go beyond the simple advantages/disadvantages exercise. Although looking at advantages to accepting and disadvantages to not accepting is good, it doesn't reveal the hidden payoffs to not doing anything. If these hidden payoffs are not recognized, it can sabotage decision-making. By identifying and addressing these hidden payoffs early, you can better cope with any losses or stress that accepting the situation might bring.

    By going through these exercises in order you can first catch the hidden payoffs that might sabotage your decision-making later. Then you can identify what you are giving up or what the costs are of not accepting the situation. Once you go through this thought process it is easier to accept advantages of accepting the situation and disadvantages of not accepting the situation without the hidden payoffs lurking in the background.

    Remember that "doing nothing" is not the same thing as actively accepting the situation.

    Some of your answers for the exercises might be similar, or even the same. That is fine. This is more about the thought process and what you discover than it is putting the "right" answer in the "right" box.

- **Exercise 3.7:** Review all the information you have written and decide if you want to accept this situation. If yes, continue to the next exercise. If the costs of accepting are too high and you decide not to accept the situation, and you have already decided that changing is not an option, consider leaving the situation.

  Something to remember is that although it might not be desirable to accept the situation forever, you might need a plan and time to leave the situation. If so, continue to the next exercise to determine how to accept the situation temporarily and determine how to leave the situation eventually.

- **Exercise 3.8:** Determine the steps you need to take to accept the situation. Consider both the external and internal factors related to the situation that you highlighted in Exercise 3.1. This can help you determine the external and internal steps you need to take. It can also be beneficial to add a timeframe indicating when you will complete each step.

Exercise 3-1
What situation do I want to address?

If you decided not to change the situation you picked in Chapter 2, you may want to use it here. Or pick another one of the situations you listed in the tables in Chapter 1. Describe it here in as much detail as possible. After you are done, highlight the external and internal factors to reference later.

Exercise 3-2
What is my desired result?

For the situation you identified, describe in detail your desired result.

Exercise 3-3
If I choose to do nothing, what do I gain?

For the situation you identified, describe in detail what you will gain if you do nothing.

Exercise 3-4
If I choose to accept, what do I lose?

For the situation you identified, describe in detail what you will lose if you accept the situation.

Exercise 3-5
If I choose to accept, what do I gain?

For the situation you identified, describe in detail what you will gain if you accept the situation.

Exercise 3-6
If I choose to do nothing, what do I lose?

For the situation you identified, describe in detail what you will lose if you do nothing.

Exercise 3-7
Do I want to accept the situation?

Review all the information you have written. Do you want to try to accept the situation? Why or why not? Write your reasons here.

ACCEPT IT

Exercise 3-8
What steps do I need to take to accept the situation?

If you decide to accept the situation, list the steps that you need to take to accept it. Consider both the external and internal factors you identified in Exercise 3.1. You also might want to add a timeframe.

Leave It 4

SOMETIMES CHANGING OR accepting a situation is not possible or desirable. Sometimes leaving the situation becomes the best option.

Leaving a situation can be minor. For example, if you go into a restaurant and after fifteen minutes no one has acknowledged your presence and if you do not want to accept this treatment, leave. You are not going to be able to change bad service.

Leaving a situation can also be a major decision. Deciding to get a divorce, for example, will probably be one the biggest decisions you will ever make. You might have a friendship that you need to leave because you have outgrown it or the person is no longer supportive of you. Leaving your current career or profession is another major decision. If you are in an abusive situation, personally or professionally, get the help you need to leave.

Did you notice in the chapter on changing that frequently changing a situation involved leaving? That's normal. Often one involves the other. In order to take a better job, for example, you have to leave your current job. As you read sections in this chapter, you may want to reread the corresponding sections in the chapter on change.

Although this chapter will follow the same format as the previous two, there are some situations where leaving isn't possible. We can't leave ourselves, for example. We can change or accept ourselves, who we are, but we cannot leave ourselves.

Again, the ideas in this chapter are designed to encourage you to think about yourself and your situations. They are not meant to be a comprehensive list. Use the information to think about other situations in your life that you want to address.

Professional Situations
- **PROFESSION/INDUSTRY**

Sometimes it is necessary to leave a profession or industry. Maybe it was not a good choice from the beginning. Maybe the profession or industry has changed and is no longer something that brings satisfaction. Or maybe you have changed and need something new and different.

Before making the decision to leave, though, do the research to determine whether you will gain what you want by leaving. If no, then reevaluate whether it is the profession that is causing dissatisfaction or it is something else.

If you will gain what you want by leaving your current

profession and changing to a new one, then the next step is to plan an exit strategy. Very few of us have the luxury of leaving a job, never mind a profession, without another to take its place. What do you need to do to be successful in the new profession after you leave the old? Will you need to obtain an additional degree, education, certification? How long will it take? How much will it cost? What will you need to do to tolerate the old until you can achieve the new? What is your exit strategy?

■ POSITION/JOB RESPONSIBILITIES

Sometimes it is not possible to change or accept your current position or job responsibilities and it becomes necessary to leave. Before you do, be sure it is the position and not the profession or company that is causing the dissatisfaction.

As with leaving your profession, it is necessary to have an exit plan. It may take time and work before you have positioned yourself to be able to leave.

■ COMPANY/EMPLOYER

Sometimes a company is not a good fit and the best option is to leave. As with leaving a profession or position, though, have an exit strategy. Determine what you need to do to have a position with a new company before you leave the old, and then do it.

Although I have left professions, positions, and companies, it has always been part of positive change, part of advancing my career. Although there have been things I have not liked about different professions, positions, and companies, nothing has ever been so bad that I felt I had to leave.

In looking back, though, there were a couple of situations that had the potential to turn bad given time. Whether through luck, being proactive, or having the desire to continually advance, I had moved on before things reached the point of where I would have felt that I had to leave. It can be beneficial to keep yourself marketable so that you can move to new opportunities before you need to leave the current situation.

▪ INTERNAL FACTORS

If you have an unsatisfactory professional situation that you cannot change and that you cannot accept, the alternative is leaving the situation. If you know this, but are reluctant to leave, why? What internal factors might be keeping you from leaving?

Do you not want to leave because of fear? Fear of change? Fear of the unknown? Fear that you might find yourself in a worse situation? Fear that you will find yourself in a worse financial situation? Fear of failure?

Do you not want to leave out of pride or ego? Have you invested so much into your career that you do not want to admit that you made a mistake? Will you feel embarrassed if you leave? Are you worried that people will judge you if you leave? Is it a matter of stubbornness? Do you see leaving as a sign of failure? What are your beliefs about these possible internal factors?

If you are reluctant to leave a bad situation, determining why can help you make a better decision. The exercises at the end of this chapter can assist you in discovering internal factors that might be hindering you.

There are people who are reluctant to leave a situation.

There are also people who leave situations quickly and frequently, perhaps when either changing or accepting a situation might have been a better choice. If you find that you leave positions, jobs, or professions frequently, you might want to ask yourself why.

It's one thing to leave frequently when each time it is part of your plan to advance your career. It's another thing if it's a form of running away. When you leave, is it for growth? Or is it giving up? At the time, does it seem easier to leave than to address the situation? Does it seem easier to leave than to confront someone? Or possibly confront yourself? Do you think this is best in the long run?

Personal Situations
- **RELATIONSHIP STATUS**

As with professional situations, before you can change your relationship status you need to leave the one you are in. For example, once you marry, you are no longer single. Generally, when we think of leaving a relationship, however, we think of a break-up or divorce. That will be the focus of this section.

Sometimes a relationship cannot be changed because the other person will not change. And we can no longer accept the way the relationship affects our life. It's a serious decision, but it's one that sometimes needs to be made for our own physical, mental, and/or emotional health. As difficult as it is, though, often this is what we need to do to improve our future.

In some ways, leaving a relationship is similar to leaving a professional situation. Identify why you want to leave and what you hope to gain by leaving. You may need to plan an exit strategy. If you do not have an income of your own, and are financially dependent upon your spouse, it can be more difficult to leave. Is there anything you need to do before you can leave? If you are in a more serious situation, such as domestic violence, seek the help you need to be able to leave. There are resources available.

> I have gone through a divorce. I'll talk more about it in a subsequent chapter as it demonstrates how we often try to change and accept things first and when neither works all we are left with is leaving.

▪ PARENTHOOD (OR NOT)

Can you leave parenthood? Or once a parent, always a parent? I'm not sure. The only example of leaving parenthood that I can think of is if you give a child up for adoption. In this case, you would turn over all responsibility for the child to another who wants that responsibility. This is a situation where it might be the best for you and the child.

In the case of divorce, you are still a parent, and most people I know still act like parents. Something that I have heard frequently is that the person divorced his or her spouse, not the children. It is certainly possible to be a great parent, even if you are not married to your child's other parent.

If you abandon your child and have nothing to do with him or her, in my opinion you are still a parent: not a good one, but still a parent.

It is extremely important to determine why you want children, why you want to be a parent, before becoming a parent. Having a child is not like adopting a pet from the humane society. If it doesn't work, you can't give her or him back. Becoming a parent is probably the most important, and most far-reaching, decision you will ever make. Be sure it is for the right reasons. Also, be sure your partner is in full agreement. It will be his child, too. Parenthood is too important to be forced upon anyone.

▪ INTERESTS

As stated before, our interests and hobbies are those things that add to our lives in some way. If any of them get to be too much, we can generally stop doing them with no, or minimal, consequences. We can also decide to set them aside and pick them up again later when we have more time.

> I learned how to knit and crochet when I was a child. It's something I enjoy doing, but usually it is not very high on my priority list. I may not knit or crochet anything for years, but it is always something I can start again when I want.

▪ INTERNAL FACTORS

The reasons for not leaving a professional situation (fear, pride, ego, embarrassment, feelings of failure) can apply to personal situations as well.

If you are reluctant to leave a relationship, ask yourself whether it is out of fear. It could be out of fear of the unknown, fear of being alone, fear of being unable to financially support yourself, fear of what others will say.

Unfortunately, there are many circles that promote the perceived necessity of being in a relationship. Although in society in general there is not the same stigma attached to being divorced as there once was, you might be in a situation where divorce is strongly discouraged. Examine your beliefs and where they originated. Does it make sense for who you are today to stay in a bad relationship? Is that how you want to live your life? Are you willing to sacrifice the life you desire because of one bad mistake? Or would it be better to correct that mistake and move on?

As with professional situations, there are some people who don't leave when it would probably be better if they did. And there are others who leave situations when it might be better to try to change or accept the situation.

If you are continually leaving relationships, ask yourself why. Is out of fear of commitment or fear of failure? Could it be related to unrealistic expectations of others? Is it a method of avoiding conflict?

The exercises at the end of the chapter can assist you in determining internal factors related to leaving.

Overall Wellness

▪ HEALTH

Although we can change our health, we cannot leave "health." Our health may be good or poor, and we can change the way it is or accept it, but we cannot leave it.

▪ APPEARANCE

Appearance, like health, is something that we have. We will always have an appearance of some sort. We can change our appearance or accept it, but we cannot leave it.

▪ TIME

Time is another issue that we cannot leave. We all have the same amount of time each day, and all we can do is change how we use it or accept how we use it.

- **FINANCES**

Like lifestyle, the only way we can leave our financial situation is to change it. We will always have a financial situation. Whether it is billionaire status or destitute, we will have one.

- **RELATIONSHIPS**

We frequently leave relationships. Often we don't even consciously leave them: we just don't put the effort into maintaining them and they fade away. How many friends do you have now who were also friends in high school? College? Former jobs? If not many, that isn't necessarily a bad thing. We change, they change, and sometimes what brought us together in the past isn't enough to hold us together now. That's part of life.

There are other relationships, though, that we choose to leave. Professionally, if you choose to leave a job you are also choosing to leave the people at the job such as your supervisor, employees, and co-workers. You may create new relationships with them outside of the job, or you may not. You may choose to "leave" relationships with customers or suppliers if it is no longer good to do business with them. Whenever possible, it is a good idea to leave these relationships as positively as possible. You never know if you might want to recreate a relationship with them later.

Of course, there are times when leaving a relationship is difficult. Sometimes we outgrow a friendship, or grow in different directions from that person and we don't have that much in common anymore. If it gets to the point that you make time for someone because you feel obligated or guilty rather than because you want to spend time with them, maybe it's time to leave the friendship. It may be that you like someone, but it isn't good for you to be around him or her. Negative people are a good example. If there is someone who makes you feel worse just by being around her, question why you still have her as a friend. If the relationship has turned abusive, it's time to leave.

Sometimes it is not possible to entirely "leave" certain people, but you can at least minimize the time you spend with them and the negative impact they have on you. Family members can fall into this category. There are probably a few that you will need to tolerate, at least occasionally. Then it becomes a matter of managing the situation so that it has the least negative impact on you.

I am one of those people who prefer having a few close friends. I have many professional associates and am happy to see them when I do. However, if life takes us in different directions, I don't go out of my way to stay in touch. Because I try to keep my relationships positive, if I meet them again it's usually a positive experience and often we can pick up from where we left off.

▪ LIFESTYLE

The only way to leave our lifestyle is to change it. It's not as though we can live without a lifestyle. As long as we are living, we have a lifestyle of one sort or another. If there are aspects of your lifestyle that you do not like, evaluate why, determine what you want to change, develop a plan to make the changes, and implement the plan. Or accept your lifestyle, or aspects of it, as it is.

- **INTERNAL FACTORS**

Technically, if we have a functioning brain, we cannot "leave" thoughts or beliefs in that we cannot stop having them. We will always have thoughts and beliefs and can only replace old with new.

I think it is more empowering, however, to think of leaving the old behind us so that it does not have power or control over us. We can choose to leave negative thoughts behind us. We can choose to leave self-limiting beliefs behind us. We can choose not to let the past live in our present or be part of our future. We can choose positive and empowering thoughts and beliefs.

If you do not want to leave a situation, even though neither changing nor accepting is a good option, ask yourself why. The information and questions in the professional and personal sections apply here as well.

If you tend to leave situations too readily without trying to change them first, determining why can assist you in making better decisions.

Summary

There are some things that we cannot leave, we can only change them or accept them. Health, lifestyle, appearance, and financial status are all examples.

There are other things that we can leave, such as people (relationships) and some professional and personal situations. Sometimes leaving is minor, sometimes not. In major situations, it might be necessary to have an exit strategy in place before leaving. Then it is a matter of learning how to accept the situation until you can leave it. In serious situations, seeking professional help can be extremely beneficial.

Exercises

The following exercises are designed to help you decide whether you want to leave a situation.

- **Exercise 4.1:** If you chose not to change or accept the previous situation, use it for this exercise. You can evaluate as many situations for changing or accepting as you want before moving to this exercise. Whichever situation you pick, describe it here in as much detail as possible. Remember to include external and internal factors. Use the highlighters to indicate each.

- **Exercise 4.2:** Describe in as much detail as possible your desired result. What outcome do you want by leaving the situation? The more specific you can be, the more likely you are to achieve a satisfying result.

- **Exercises 4.3–4.6:** These exercises go beyond the simple advantages/disadvantages exercise. Although looking at advantages to leaving and disadvantages to not leaving is good, it doesn't reveal the hidden payoffs to not doing anything. If these hidden payoffs are not recognized, it can sabotage decision-making. By identifying and addressing these hidden payoffs early, you can better cope with any losses or stress that leaving the situation might bring.

  By going through these exercises in order you can first catch the hidden payoffs that might sabotage your decision-making later. Then you can identify what you are giving up or what the costs are of not leaving the situation. Once you go through this thought process it is easier to accept advantages of leaving the situation and disadvantages of not leaving the situation without the hidden payoffs lurking in the background.

Some of your answers for the exercises might be similar, or even the same. That is fine. This is more about the thought process and what you discover than it is putting the "right" answer in the "right" box.

- **Exercise 4.7:** Review all the information you have written and decide if you want to leave this situation. If yes, continue to the next exercise. If the costs of leaving are too high and you decide not to leave the situation, go back and reevaluate how you can change or accept the situation.

- **Exercise 4.8:** Determine the steps you need to take to leave the situation. Consider both external and internal factors related to the situation that you identified in Exercise 4.1. This can help you determine the external and internal steps you need to take. It can also be beneficial to add a timeframe indicating when you will complete each step.

If it will take time to leave the situation, go back to the previous chapter and see if you can find a way to temporarily accept the situation until you can leave.

4 — LEAVE IT

Exercise 4-1
What situation do I want to address?

If you decided not to change or accept the situation you picked previously, you may want to use it here. Or pick another one of the situations you listed in the tables in Chapter 1. Describe it here in as much detail as possible. After you are done, highlight the external and internal factors to reference later.

Exercise 4-2
What is my desired result?

For the situation you identified, describe in detail your desired result.

4 — CHANGE IT · ACCEPT IT · **LEAVE IT**

Exercise 4-3
If I choose to do nothing, what do I gain?

For the situation you identified, describe in detail what you will gain if you do nothing.

Exercise 4-4
If I choose to leave, what do I lose?

For the situation you identified, describe in detail what you will lose if you leave the situation.

4 — LEAVE IT

Exercise 4-5
If I choose to leave, what do I gain?

For the situation you identified, describe in detail what you will gain if you leave the situation.

Exercise 4-6
If I choose to do nothing, what do I lose?

For the situation you identified, describe in detail what you will lose if you do nothing.

4

LEAVE IT

Exercise 4-7
Do I want to leave the situation?

Review all the information you have written. Do you want to leave the situation? Why or why not? Write your reasons here.

Exercise 4-8
What steps do I need to take to leave the situation?

If you decide to leave the situation, list the steps that you need to take to leave it. Consider both the external and internal factors you identified in Exercise 4.1. You also might want to add a timeframe.

Poor Choices 5

WE HAVE DISCUSSED how there are generally three good choices to any situation: change it, accept it, or leave it. We need to decide which choice is the best in each situation. Depending on the situation, of course, there might be only one good choice. If the situation is abusive, for example, the only good choice might be to leave.

There are many poor choices available in any situation as well. These poor choices are ineffective behaviors, ineffective coping strategies. They hinder us, they do not help us.

Some ineffective behaviors are discussed in this chapter. Please keep in mind that this is not a comprehensive list or a comprehensive discussion of those items that are mentioned. The intent is to provide enough information for you to start thinking about whether you are making poor choices. If so, I encourage you to do your own research to learn more about ineffective coping strategies. There are many books and articles available to assist you. As you learn more, you might even want to consider professional help.

Apathy

Apathy is a lack of interest, concern, or enthusiasm. You know you should do something, but you just don't have the energy to do it. Rather than make a choice to change, accept, or leave a situation, you do nothing because it does not seem worth the effort. You don't care enough to try to do anything.

It's important to try to determine why you feel this way. Did something happen that makes you feel that no matter what you do, you can't win? You can't succeed? You can't make a difference? Is it something, or a series of somethings, that has happened recently? Or is this a result of childhood programming where no matter what you did, it wasn't good enough?

If you can determine why you feel this way, then you can do something about it. Can you change your attitude and focus on your achievements rather than your perceived failures? Is there something, anything, that you can do at this moment to get you moving toward a solution to the situation you are facing?

If apathy is something that you face in most or all aspects of your life, not just a situation or two with which you are dissatisfied, you might want to seek professional help.

Choosing to Do Nothing

We always make choices. Sometimes people think a situation is out of their control, so they do nothing. Sometimes they think that if they do nothing, the situation will no longer be their responsibility, but it still is. Doing nothing is a choice. Choosing not to choose is still a choice.

When we choose to do nothing, nothing changes. The situation that we are not satisfied with is still the same, it doesn't change. Our outlook or perception of the situation doesn't change, either.

Complaining

Venting is a way to release frustration. There is nothing wrong with venting, feeling better, and then doing something constructive about the situation. The problem is when simple venting turns into chronic complaining. If weeks, months, years, or even decades have passed and you are still venting—it's not venting.

It is all too easy to complain about things. However, complaining takes time and energy without any positive results. We might as well use that time and energy to do something about the situation. We can work on changing it, accepting it, or leaving it. At least then we will have accomplished something. Complaining does not accomplish anything.

> I have known people, and I am sure you have as well, who have wasted time and energy complaining instead of doing something positive about a situation. I have also known people who decide to leave a situation and implement a plan to do so, but rather than accept the situation until they can leave, they continue to waste energy by complaining about it. I often wonder whether they could have left the situation sooner if they had focused all their energy on leaving rather than diverting their energy into complaining.

Denial

Short-term denial can be a good thing. It can be a coping mechanism to give us the time we need to adjust to distressing or disturbing situations. Staying in denial about a situation, though, does not help us. It keeps us from moving forward and dealing with the situation. It is important that we remember that denial is only a temporary measure, it does not change reality. If we do not face reality and deal with it, our problems can spiral out of control.

Excessive Worrying

A certain amount of worry can be good. For example, if we are a little worried about our finances, we might control our spending better. However, excessive worrying can negatively impact our lives. It not only has mental and emotional consequences, it can also have an impact on our physical well-being.

Worrying alone does not change anything, it does not solve anything. It takes time and energy without providing anything productive in return. Excessive worrying can be paralyzing. If excessive worrying is preventing you from making changes in your life, this is something to address.

> I worry. I worry that I worry too much. I always have. What I have found that helps me is that when I realize that I am worrying about something, I develop the worst-case scenario in my mind and then develop a plan to address it. What is the worst thing that could happen? If it does, what am I going to do about it? As soon as I do this, most of the time I realize that what I am worrying about isn't that big of deal. And even if it is, as long as I have a plan, even if the plan is that "I'll survive," then

I'm okay. Then I can move forward despite the worry. It's as though having a plan gives me control of the situation again.

Giving Up

Sometimes people decide they are going to try to change, accept, or leave a situation and when it becomes difficult, they give up. They might give up before even trying very hard, or they might put some effort into it and then give up too soon. They abandon what they intended to do. It is important to be persistent. Things rarely work without persistence and determination.

It is also important, however, to know when something is not working and then develop a new plan. This might be using a new tactic or method. This is not the same thing as giving up.

Holding a Grudge

Holding a grudge is ineffective. You cannot change, accept, or even leave a situation while holding a grudge. (You may have left a person or a place. But if you are still holding a grudge, you have not left the situation—it still controls you.) Holding grudges only hurts you, not the object of your grudge.

> Several years ago, I was working as a consultant in long-term care facilities. I was working with a dietary manager to improve meal service. There were a few items I wanted to discuss with the dietitian. The manager told me that the dietitian would not talk to me. Why? Apparently, many years prior to that she wanted a promotion that I could give. I do not

remember her applying for that position, and yet somehow it was my fault that I did not intuitively know that she wanted it and offer it to her. She had carried this around with her for almost 20 years. It certainly did not hurt me; I didn't even know about it. But think about the damage it did to her to hold on to a grudge for that long.

Not Taking Responsibility

Not taking responsibility is another ineffective behavior.

One aspect of not taking responsibility is to blame others. We are all responsible for the choices we make and the consequences of these choices. When we blame others, we are trying to pass on our responsibility. It doesn't work this way. All we are doing is giving away our power and control over the situation. Only when we take responsibility, when we take ownership, do we have power and control.

Another aspect of not taking responsibility is to expect others to fix our problems, to bail us out of trouble. It's not their responsibility to do that. It's our responsibility. But if we expect others to fix our problems, and wait around for them to do it (which they might not), we are again giving away our power and our control over our lives.

Passive-Aggressive Behavior

Passive-aggressive behavior is the indirect expression of anger or hostility. There is a disconnect between what is said and what is done. Rather than be assertive and confront someone, we are passive to their face, and aggressive behind their back.

For example, someone who is passive-aggressive to her

supervisor might pleasantly agree to take on a new project, even though she doesn't feel she has time, but then gives one excuse after another on why it doesn't get done. This behavior ends up hurting the employee, because she creates a reputation of not completing assignments in a timely way. A better solution would be for her to tell her supervisor that she doesn't currently have time for the new project but would be willing to discuss options so the project is completed, such as someone else taking some of her existing work or establishing a later deadline.

Passive-aggressive behavior also happens in our personal lives. If we are annoyed that our spouse or partner is spending what we think is too much time on personal hobbies, it is better to address that with him or her than it is to give the silent treatment.

It can be easy to fall into passive-aggressive behavior. It can take careful analysis of what we are doing, and why we are doing it, to identify it. It might also take professional help to identify and change it.

Self-Destructive Behaviors

There are many self-destructive behaviors. These can include smoking, alcohol and drug abuse, overeating, compulsive computer-gaming, self-injury, and many other behaviors that feel good at the moment but can have devastating effects long-term.

Doing these things does not change the situation that a person is facing. Someone might have started doing these things to try to deal with a painful situation, but it does not change the situation. These are all ineffective, even destructive, coping mechanisms.

Another Consideration

Although not exactly a poor choice, there is something else that I want to mention because it deserves consideration. We do not make choices in a vacuum. Neither does anyone else.

We often make our choices based upon the choices other people make. This might or might not be good, depending upon the situation. Be aware of this and think about all the reasons you are making a choice.

Others often make choices based upon the choices we make. Again, depending upon the situation, this might or might not be good. For example, people will probably choose to treat us the way we choose to treat them. If we choose to treat people with dignity and respect, they are more likely to treat us the same way. Think about how your choices affect other people and how that in turn affects their choices involving you.

Summary

Although there are generally three good choices for any situation, there are also numerous poor choices. These poor choices are ineffective coping strategies or ineffective behaviors. Some of these poor choices have been discussed briefly here. If you think you are making any of these, or if there is something that you are doing that is not working for you, investigate it, research it.

Poor choices have costs associated with them. At a minimum, they keep us from moving forward. This costs us time, energy, and often money. It keeps us from the enjoyment we could have if we made a positive choice and moved on. It keeps us from the success that we deserve.

Exercises

The following tables are designed to assist you in determining whether you are wasting time and energy on ineffective behaviors and, if so, whether you want to change.

- **Exercise 5.1:** Pick an ineffective behavior that you want to address. Describe it in as much detail as possible.

- **Exercise 5.2:** Describe in as much detail as possible your desired result. What outcome do you want? The more specific you can be, the more likely you are to achieve a satisfying result.

- **Exercises 5.3–5.6:** These exercises go beyond the simple advantages/disadvantages exercise. Although looking at advantages to changing an ineffective behavior and disadvantages to not changing an ineffective behavior is good, it doesn't reveal the hidden payoffs to staying the same. If these hidden payoffs are not recognized, they can sabotage decision-making. By identifying and addressing these hidden payoffs early, you can better cope with any losses or stress that change might bring.

  By going through these exercises in order you can first catch the hidden payoffs that might sabotage your decision-making later. Then you can identify what you are giving up or what the costs are of not changing. Once you go through this thought process it is easier to accept advantages of changing ineffective behaviors and disadvantages of not changing ineffective behaviors without the hidden payoffs lurking in the background.

Some of your answers for the exercises might be similar, or even the same. That is fine. This is more about the thought process and what you discover than it is putting the "right" answer in the "right" box.

- **Exercise 5.7:** Review all the information you have written and decide whether you want to change an ineffective behavior. If you decide to change, continue to the next exercise. If the costs of changing are too high and you decide not to change, then find a way to accept the costs that go along with this decision.

- **Exercise 5.8:** Determine the steps you need to take to change your ineffective behavior. They might include doing additional research or seeking professional assistance.

Exercise 5-1
What ineffective behavior do I want to address?

Describe it here in as much detail as possible.

5 POOR CHOICES

5 POOR CHOICES

Exercise 5-2
What is my desired result?

For the ineffective behavior you identified, describe in detail your desired result.

Exercise 5-3
If I choose to do nothing, what do I gain?

For the ineffective behavior you identified, describe in detail what you will gain if you do nothing.

5 POOR CHOICES

Exercise 5-4
If I choose to change, what do I lose?

For the ineffective behavior you identified, describe in detail what you will lose if you change.

Exercise 5-5
If I choose to change, what do I gain?

For the ineffective behavior you identified, describe in detail what you will gain if you change.

5 POOR CHOICES

Exercise 5-6
If I choose to do nothing, what do I lose?

For the ineffective behavior you identified, describe in detail what you will lose if you do nothing.

Exercise 5-7
Do I want to change the ineffective behavior?

Review all the information you have written. Do you want to try to change? Why or why not? Write your reasons here.

5 POOR CHOICES

Exercise 5-8
What steps do I need to take to change the ineffective behavior?

If you decide to change, list the steps that you need to take to change.

Rights and Responsibility   6

WE ALL HAVE rights. We have some rights simply because we are human, such as the right to be treated with dignity and respect. We have some rights because of where we live. For example, in the United States we have rights as regulated by federal, state, and local laws. We also have earned rights. For example, we have earned the right to a certain salary with a company because of our education, knowledge, skills, experience, and/or accomplishments.

With these rights come responsibilities. We have personal responsibilities--responsibilities to ourselves. We also have interpersonal responsibilities--responsibilities to others.

The challenge is to balance rights and responsibilities.

How do we stand up for our rights without infringing upon the rights of others? How do we ensure that others

6 RIGHTS AND RESPONSIBILITIES

respect our rights? If you are in an abusive situation, or if standing up for your rights may have serious consequences, you might want to seek professional help.

How do we meet our personal responsibilities when they conflict with our interpersonal responsibilities? How do we balance our responsibilities to ourselves and our responsibilities to our spouse/partner, children, parents, friends, employer, co-workers, etc.?

Frequently, there are not any easy answers. The following is provided to give you a few ideas for reflection related to choices.

We have the right to make our own choices. We do not have the right to make choices that harm others, however, just as they do not have the right to make choices to harm us. (If you are in a situation that is harmful to you physically, mentally, or emotionally, seek professional help.)

Harm can come in many forms. For example, if you routinely overspend on the family budget to buy the things you want, that can cause harm for your partner because then there is not the money for the things that you agreed upon. Bringing home a pet without agreement can cause harm because it causes lifestyle changes. And, of course, getting pregnant intentionally without your partner's agreement causes harm for him because it changes his life forever. It also causes harm for the child because he or she is brought into the world without being completely wanted by both parents. Ultimately, it can harm you, too.

Another way to view this is to ask yourself how you would feel if your partner made decisions that changed your life without discussing it with you first. And if your partner is doing this, it is probably a situation you will want to address.

Generally, we do not have the right to make choices for others, just as they do not have the right to make choices for us. We might, as a courtesy, order a drink for our friend if we know what she likes to drink and she hasn't arrived yet. If you consistently make choices for someone, however, look at why. Is it manipulation? Control? Forced dependency? Why aren't you letting them make their own choices? If the reverse is true and you consistently let others make choices for you, evaluate why you let them do this. Are these good reasons?

If you are a parent, then you are responsible for making choices for your children and taking responsibility for them. As they grow older, you give them more rights (including making choices) as they prove they can take on more responsibility. Something to ask yourself is why you are making the choices you are. Is it to benefit them or you? For example, buying them whatever they want may make you happy. But it is teaching them instant gratification, which will not help them as they get older. As another example, if you are doing things for them that they could do for themselves, is it to help them or is it to keep them dependent upon you? If it is your way of showing love, is there another way that you can show love and foster self-sufficiency?

In any situation, it is our responsibility to decide what we are going to do. (Remember, choosing to do nothing is also a choice.) No one can change, accept, or leave a situation for us. We must do it ourselves and that starts with taking the responsibility to do it. No one can make choices for us. Even if we decide to go along with what someone else says, we are still choosing to do that.

We are also responsible for the consequences of our choices. If the consequences are positive, then we can take credit for that. If the consequences are negative, we still must take responsibility for them and decide what we are going to do next.

Taking responsibility is empowering. When we take responsibility for ourselves, our lives, our decisions, our actions, we have control over our lives. We are keeping our power. When we try to make other people responsible for us, we are giving away our power. We are giving them control over us.

An indication that we are not taking responsibility is when we blame others. If we tell ourselves that some aspect of our lives is caused by someone else, because of what someone else has done, that is inaccurate. Ultimately, our life is an accumulation of our choices, thoughts, and actions.

We cannot control what happens to us, but we always control how we respond. For example, if we tell ourselves we can't get a raise because our boss is a jerk, and stop there, we are giving away our power. If we take responsibility for what we can do, and decide whether to change, accept, or leave our job, then we are keeping and using our power. Many bosses are jerks, but that doesn't mean we can't do something to get paid more.

Remember that balancing personal and interpersonal responsibilities can be difficult. One thing that can make it easier is clear communication. Tell the other person what you expect from him or her and listen to what he or she expects from you. Another important aspect is respect. Respect yourself, respect the other person, and set the expectation that the other person will respect you.

I am fortunate that my parents raised my brothers and me to be responsible. We learned from a very early age that there were consequences to our choices and actions. Positive choices and actions were rewarded and negative ones were not. As an example, when it came to school, we were expected to get good grades. (As far as my father was concerned, "A" was for "average" so we should get A's. For the most part, we did.) If we didn't get a grade that was as good as it could have been, we were never asked what the teacher did. We were asked what we did or did not do. Did we study enough? Did we do the homework? Could we have done it better? We could never blame our grade on our teacher. Our grade was the result of our actions. At the time, I could not imagine what an important lesson that was.

Exercises

The following exercises are designed to help you determine whether you want to take more responsibility for your life.

- **Exercise 6.1:** Describe in as much detail as possible an area in your life (or a situation you are facing) where you would like to take more responsibility, or where you think it would be beneficial to take more responsibility.

- **Exercise 6.2:** Describe in as much detail as possible your desired result.

- **Exercises 6.3–6.6:** These exercises go beyond the simple advantages/disadvantages exercise. Although looking at advantages to taking greater responsibility and disadvantages to not taking more responsibility is good, it doesn't reveal the hidden payoffs to staying the same. If these hidden payoffs are not recognized, they can sabotage decision-making. By identifying and addressing these hidden payoffs early, you can better cope with any losses or stress that change might bring.

By going through these exercises in order you can first catch the hidden payoffs that might sabotage your decision-making later. Then you can identify what you are giving up or what the costs are of not changing. Once you go through this thought process it is easier to accept advantages of changing and disadvantages of not changing without the hidden payoffs lurking in the background.

Some of your answers for the exercises might be similar, or even the same. That is fine. This is more about the thought process and what you discover than it is putting the "right" answer in the "right" box.

- **Exercise 6.7:** Review all the information you have written and decide whether you want to take additional responsibility. If yes, then continue to the next exercise.

- **Exercise 6.8:** Determine the steps needed for you to take more responsibility.

Exercise 6-1
What area of my life/situation do I want to address?

Describe it here in as much detail as possible.

Exercise 6-2
What is my desired result?

Describe in detail your desired result.

Exercise 6-3
If I choose to do nothing, what do I gain?

Describe in detail what you will gain if you do nothing.

RIGHTS AND RESPONSIBILITIES

Exercise 6-4
If I choose to change, what do I lose?

Describe in detail what you will lose if you change the situation.

Exercise 6-5
If I choose to change, what do I gain?

Describe in detail what you will gain if you change the situation.

RIGHTS AND RESPONSIBILITIES

6

Exercise 6-6
If I choose to do nothing, what do I lose?

Describe in detail what you will lose if you do nothing.

Exercise 6-7
Do I want to change?

Review all the information you have written. Do you want to take more responsibility for your life? Why or why not? Write your reasons here.

RIGHTS AND RESPONSIBILITIES

Exercise 6-8
What steps do I need to take to change?

If you decide to change, list the steps that you need to take.

Conclusion

ALTHOUGH THIS BOOK discusses making choices as a linear process (first change, and if that doesn't work, accept, and if that doesn't work, leave) in reality the process is usually more convoluted. It might resemble a swirl or zig-zag more than a straight line. This is especially true the more complicated the situation is. There is not any right or wrong way on how your process looks: the important thing is that you make the best choice you can with the information you have at the time.

I am going to use my relationship with my ex-husband as an example of how this process can be used and how it can be a convoluted process rather than a linear one.

We started dating when I was 16 and he was 17. Although I never felt pressure from my parents or extended family to date

CONCLUSION

(my parents probably would have preferred that I not date until I was 30, or at least finished with college and established in a career), there was still pressure from peers and society to get a boyfriend. So I did. Which, I realize now, was not a very good reason.

We dated through high school and into college. In my junior year of college, we started living together and continued after I graduated. After ten years together, it seemed time to marry. This, also, was not a very good reason. After approximately five years of marriage we divorced, at my request.

He wasn't a bad person, and it wasn't a bad relationship. It just wasn't what I wanted in a partner or relationship. I wanted someone more like me: ambitious, motivated, responsible, and independent. For example, it took him longer to achieve a two-year associate degree than it took me to achieve two bachelor's degrees, with a minor, and an internship. Although he worked, he really would have preferred to stay at home and be a house husband. I was constantly working for the next promotion. I was the one who decided it was time to buy a house. I saved the money for the down payment, built the good credit rating to get a loan, and paid the mortgage.

It took me almost 15 years to realize that I wanted an equal partner and he wanted a provider.

During those years, I fluctuated between accepting what I had and trying to change him. When I was in the accepting mode, I told myself that it wasn't that bad and tried to be satisfied and happy with what I had. That never lasted very long. When I was trying to change him I was frustrated because, of course, he didn't change.

When I finally acknowledged that I could not change him and that I could no longer accept my life as it was, I started thinking about divorce. The deciding factor for me was when I imagined myself at age 90 looking back on my life and the decision I had made. The best possible outcome would be if I found the partner and relationship that I wanted. To do that I would need to obtain a divorce to get my freedom back and search for what I wanted.

There were, of course, other possible outcomes. One was that I get a divorce, look, and not find anyone. Another was that I stay married and never know what I could have had, what my life could have been like. I realized that the last would have been the worst. Living my life not knowing what could have happened if I had taken the risk was unacceptable.

Again, he wasn't a bad person. It just wasn't a good match.

I'm very glad I made the difficult decision to leave the situation. I found what I wanted. I have a wonderful partnership with someone who is an equal partner to me and sees me as an equal partner as well. I love him and our life together more than I could ever have imagined possible.

Although leaving my first marriage was the right choice for me, it might not have been the right choice for anyone else. It is essential that each of us makes the right choice for us, not for someone else. Whether we choose to change, accept, or leave a situation, it must be right for us. And although we may bounce back and forth between choices, at some point we must make a final decision and embrace it.

The following table is designed to assist you in taking all that you have done with the previous tables and summarizing what you will do. You can make it as simple or as detailed as you like.

Whatever you decide, I wish you all the best in your life.

CONCLUSION

Exercise 7-1

Review what you have written in the previous exercises. Summarize here what you want and what you will do to achieve it.

Author's Note

I would love to see a second edition of this book filled with stories from readers about choices that they have made.

If you have a story that you would like to share, please email it to me at **Susan@SusanLFarrell.com**.

I would also like to know what you liked about the book and whether there was anything you did not like about the book. I am constantly trying to improve myself and my work. Your comments would be greatly appreciated.

Please go to my website, **SusanLFarrell.com**, for additional information and to order additional products.

Thank you, and the best to you in your journey toward self-empowerment!

Susan L. Farrell

Acknowledgments

Thank you to my husband, **Rick**, for his support, understanding, and patience.

Thank you to my cousin and friend, **Pat Olson**, for her copyediting, proofreading, and insightful suggestions.

Thank you to **Amy Gurka, Ph.D.**, Clinical Psychologist, for her phenomenal conceptual suggestions as content editor.

Thank you to **Andrew Welyczko** for the beautiful interior and cover design as well as his never-ending patience.

Thank you to **Shannon Crotty** for writing the foreword and for creating Polka Dot Powerhouse, the most supportive association I have ever belonging to.

And thank you to my immediate and extended families for their support and encouragement.

About the Author

SUSAN HAS ALWAYS loved to learn. One BS in college was not enough; she obtained a double major with a minor. Years later, she returned to college for an MBA. Susan also believes deeply in learning everything possible from personal and professional experiences.

Her first career out of college was with a national health care company. She quickly moved from the facility level to division, field, and corporate levels. When she left she had been an executive director with national responsibilities for several years.

As owner of SLF Consulting & Training, LLC, Susan assisted clients with the challenges of combining customer satisfaction, cost control, and regulatory compliance. Her business acumen made her a sought-after speaker which led

ABOUT THE AUTHOR

to a successful speaking career. This, in turn, led to her current writing career on self-empowerment for women.

A normal extension of a love of learning is a love of teaching. Susan has accomplished this in various positions through teaching and training her employees, co-workers, associates, and customers. She has taught as an adjunct instructor at business colleges. She has informally coached employees, associates, and friends in advancing professionally and personally. She now assists others through her books, blogs, and newsletter.

She is the author of *Don't Act Like Prey! A Woman's Guide to Self-Empowerment*, a book on respectful assertiveness as an option to passive or aggressive behavior. *52 Weeks of Wisdom, A Woman's Guide to Self-Empowerment*, is designed to provide ideas to encourage women to think about what they do, why they do it, and do they want to change. *3 Good Choices: Change It, Accept It, or Leave It; A Woman's Guide to Self-Empowerment* discusses how to make positive choices in all aspects of life.

Susan lives in rural Wisconsin with her husband and three cats.

www.ingramcontent.com/pod-product-compliance
Lightning Source LLC
LaVergne TN
LVHW051601070426
835507LV00021B/2711